The Art
of Making
WINE

The Art
of Making
WINE

Stanley F. Anderson
with Raymond Hull

HAWTHORN BOOKS, INC.
Publishers   New York

THE ART OF MAKING WINE

1 2 3 4 5 6 7 8 9 10

CONTENTS

The Instant Winemaker

If you have just acquired an unexpected lot of fruit and want to start making wine with it right away before it spoils, see the Emergency Guide on page 173.

ACKNOWLEDGMENT

I would like to acknowledge the extensive help and inspiration received from the internationally-known Enologist Mrs. S. M. Tritton, M.P.S., F.R.I.C.

During the ten years of our business association, she has generously made the results of her continuing research available to amateurs all over the world. She has pointed out the pitfalls and the advantages of amateur winemaking in her several books and scientific papers.

Specifically, Mrs. Tritton was the first to publish the "Pearson Square," and the rhubarb wine recipe on page 69. Further, all our fruit wine recipes are based in part on research done by Mrs. Tritton.

Stanley F. Anderson

The Art
of Making
WINE

1. Wines and Winemaking

In Greek legend, Dionysus (called Bacchus by the Romans), the son of Zeus, first invented wine, on Mount Nysa in Libya. Thence vine culture crossed the Mediterranean to Crete and Greece, where ritual wine-drinking became part of the Dionysian cult.

The Bible reports that Noah invented the arts of viniculture and winemaking after the Flood.

Wherever wine did originate, man has for thousands of years used it as a beverage, as a medicine—it is a tranquillizer, a tonic and a soporific—and as a religious symbol.

"Wine," narrowly defined, means only the fermented juice of the *vinifera* grape. But the word may also be qualified by the name of a fruit or flower, for example, blackberry wine, dandelion wine.

The name "wine" is not deserved by those concoctions you see around Christmas-time—a mess of half-rotted pulp, sugar and water, gulped down while it's still fermenting. But a beverage made from any fruit is entitled to the name of wine so long as it has an acceptable alcoholic content and is properly aged to give it good flavour and colour.

CLASSIFICATION BY COLOUR

Wines can be grouped by colour. Red wine is self-descriptive. It is made from red grapes and such other fruits as have red juice or red skins. Most "white" wines are not white at all, but various shades of brown or yellow. Generally speaking, any wine that is not red is called "white."

Some winemakers admit, and others don't, a third colour group, the rosé (pronounced rose-ay) wines, which are neither red nor white, but pink. Rosé wines are rapidly growing in popularity.

CLASSIFICATION BY SUGAR CONTENT

Sweet wines contain 1% or more residual sugar after fermentation has stopped and the wine has aged. Some sweet wines contain as much as 14% sugar and have a noticeably syrupy taste.

"Dry" wine is the opposite of sweet wine. A dry wine should contain not more than .1% of residual sugar. It should have no sweet taste at all; its flavour should be derived solely from the alcohol and the enzymes, minerals, organic acids, esters and other trace ingredients.

As a general rule women, and men unaccustomed to wine drinking, prefer sweet wines; most men, after some experience with wine, develop a preference for the dry.

CLASSIFICATION BY USE

Certain kinds of wine have come to be favoured for certain uses. There are no hard-and-fast rules, but some combinations of wine and food have proved, by centuries of experience, to be pleasing to the average palate, and we want you to get the greatest possible pleasure from the wines that you will be making. The generally accepted uses of wine are as follows:

1. *The Aperitif* is a slightly sweet, fortified wine, meant to be drunk as an appetizer before dinner. This is the obvious place to explain what we mean by "fortifying" a wine. The ordinary fermentation process will yield only a certain proportion of alcohol—14% to 18%, depending on the strain of yeast being used. When the yeast reaches its limit of alcohol tolerance it ceases to grow, and the fermentation stops. But the winemaker can then add distilled spirits such

2

as brandy or vodka, and so raise the proportion of alcohol in the wine to 20% or more. This addition of extra alcohol is called fortification.

Sherry, Campari and Dubonnet are popular aperitifs.

2. *Table Wine* can be defined as a dry wine containing 9% to 12% alcohol by volume. As its name suggests, it is meant to be drunk with the meal. Its dryness complements the flavour of the food. You would no more want a sweet wine with your main course than you would want to sprinkle sugar on it!

White table wine, mild, fresh-tasting, reminiscent of the original fruit, goes well with light, bland foods such as fish and fowl. Red table wine, stronger in flavour, is better with meat dishes and other strong-tasting foods. For example, Chianti, a rough, strong-tasting wine, is the perfect companion for spicy Italian cooking.

Rosé is a useful compromise if you want one wine that will go with any kind of food. If it is fairly dry, it makes an acceptable table wine for all but the most discriminating drinkers.

3. *Dessert Wines* such as Sauternes, Barsac and Moselle are sweet wines which accompany the last course of a meal. They blend nicely with pastries, fruits and other such sweet dishes.

4. *After-Dinner Wines* are served when the meal is over, to be enjoyed with a cigar, a cigarette, or perhaps a nibble of cheese. These, like the aperitifs, are sweet, fortified wines. The most popular after-dinner wines are the red and white Ports. Cream Sherry, Muscatel, Angelica, Malaga, Tokay and Samos are other good after-dinner wines.

5. *Spirits* are made by distillation. Brandy is distilled from grape wine, and various liqueurs from fruit wines, such as Kirsch from cherry wine, Calvados from cider, and Slivovitz from plum wine. Home distilling is illegal. It is also dangerous, since unskilled distillation is likely to yield a beverage containing damaging quantities of methyl alcohol. This is a rank poison which can blind you or, if you get enough of it, kill you.

CLASSIFICATION BY INGREDIENTS

Most commercial wines are made from grapes, and many amateur winemakers, sooner or later, use grapes. The grape is the only fruit which contains all the ingredients, in the right proportions, for making perfect wines.

Still, many parts of the world are too cold or too hot, too wet or too dry, to grow grapes, but there's no reason to hesitate over using whatever ingredients are available locally. The following list is by no means exhaustive and is meant only to give some idea of the scope that exists for the experimentally-minded winemaker.

Cultivated fruits: apples, pears, peaches, apricots, plums, oranges, lemons, pomegranates, quinces, cranberries, blueberries, bananas.

Wild fruits: blackberries, elderberries, Oregon grapes, rose hips.

Dried fruits: raisins, figs, dates.

Fruit concentrates: grape, apricot, peach, apple, fig.

Flowers: elder-flower, dandelion, broom.

Herbs: mint, parsley, rosemary, sage, fennel.

All of these can be used in winemaking, singly or in combination. Any of the wines can be made sweet or dry, still or sparkling. You can get a wide range of colours. So you see there is scope for a lifetime's study and pleasure in winemaking.

Every winemaker should try at least some of the fruit wines. You can make wine from fresh grapes only once a year, but by using other ingredients, you can carry on your hobby all round the calendar.

COMMERCIAL WINEMAKING

Until the mid-nineteenth century, neither commercial nor home winemakers understood the fermentation process. Their methods were mainly handed down as traditions. Sometimes a lucky accident or experiment would result in an improved variety of wine; such an improvement would be guarded as a trade secret, and might make the fortune of a winery. But all too often, some unexplained disaster would spoil a batch of wine or a whole vintage.

To try and avoid these ruinous losses, Louis Pasteur, in 1857, began the first scientific study of winemaking. He observed and explained the role of wine yeast in alcoholic fermentation, and discovered how to control vinegar bacteria and other spoilage organisms.

From Pasteur's work there sprang a new, scientific wine-making technique by which commercial winemakers could consistently produce wines of any desired kind or quality. But until recently this technique was unknown to amateur winemakers. There were no books that explained it simply, no recipes that dealt in small quantities, no cultured wine yeasts on sale. Home winemakers muddled along with a mixture of luck and guesswork, in the bad old pre-Pasteur way. There's no more need for muddling; this book will show you how to become a scientific winemaker.

Let's begin by examining the production methods of the big wineries. They make enormous quantities of wine economically and reliably—they can't afford accidents when they handle thousands of gallons at a time. We can get from them some hints that will help us make good wine on a smaller scale.

Commercial wineries are usually located close to the vineyards. The wine grape flourishes best on a light soil in a warm climate. It needs a long growing season and dry summer weather. Yet excessive summer heat, such as often occurs in Southern California, the South of France and North Africa, results in a grape of high sugar content and low acidity—not the best combination for a fine-flavoured wine.

As the grape ripens, it develops a "bloom," a cloudy appearance on its skin, rather like the mist you make by breathing on a cool window-pane. The bloom is actually a fine, waxy film covered with the microscopic cells of wind-borne wild yeasts and moulds.

The ripe grapes are rushed from the vineyard to the winery and immediately crushed. The stems are removed at this stage. They contain a lot of tannin and, if left in, would make the wine bitter. The quantity of tannin in the pips is usually sufficient to make a flavourful wine.

The remaining mass of juice, pulp, skins and seeds is

called the "must." Treatment of the must at this stage determines, in many cases, the colour of the finished wine. Some grapes, such as the Alicante variety, have red juice, so they will make only red wine. But in other varieties, such as Grenache, Mission and Zinfandel, the red colour is not in the juice, but in the skins. The so-called white grapes have green or yellow skin pigment.

So at this stage, for white wine, the juice is pressed out of the must and fermented alone. For red wine, the entire must is fermented for several days, while the alcohol extracts the desired amount of pigment from the skins. Rosé wine is fermented on the skins for about twenty-four hours, then pressed out.

The sugar and acid content of the must is measured, and corrected if necessary.

In the pre-scientific winemaking era, the must was allowed to start fermenting by itself. The wild yeasts on the skins would go to work, turning the grape sugar into alcohol. But this was a chance process. There was no knowing what kinds of yeast might be present. Results could be excellent with one batch, mediocre with a second, bad with a third. Or perhaps there might not be enough wild yeast to get a strong fermentation started, in which case moulds or vinegar bacteria would take over and spoil the whole batch of must.

To eliminate risk of loss and to obtain a uniform product, modern winemakers inhibit the growth of the wild yeasts, moulds and bacteria at this stage with sulphur dioxide. This process is usually called "sulphiting."

After sulphiting, the must is inoculated with a culture of selected wine yeast. These yeasts are bred over many years, as carefully as racehorses, and chosen to give exactly the desired strength and flavour to the finished wine. A winemaker's stock of yeasts is one of his most valued assets.

A yeast "starter" has been prepared in advance, by placing some of the chosen yeast in a nutrient solution. When added to the must, it is already reproducing actively; it rapidly spreads through the entire volume of the must, and the primary fermentation begins, accompanied by the rapid generation of carbon dioxide.

The rising bubbles of gas carry with them particles of skin and pulp which float on the surface, forming what is called the "cap." This cap must be broken up from time to time. If it is allowed to dry out, it forms a favourable breeding-ground for spoilage bacteria.

The primary fermentation generates considerable heat which is drawn off, if necessary, by circulating a refrigerant through coils running through the must, or by pumping the must through cooling-coils. For red wines the temperature of the must is kept below 85°F., for white wines, below 65°F.

When the violent fermentation subsides, the liquid is drawn off and the pulp is pressed to expel all the liquid it contains. The raw wine now goes to settling vats. There, while the slow, quiet, secondary fermentation is proceeding, the coarser suspended solids slowly sink to the bottom.

The wine is "racked," meaning siphoned, into another vat, leaving behind the sediment or "lees." This racking is repeated several times. The gentle disturbance produced by racking also helps to drive off carbon dioxide, and to add a little more oxygen, which assists the secondary fermentation.

When all fermentation is finished, the wine may be treated with "finings," substances such as bentonite clay, gelatin or isinglass which precipitate any remaining suspended matter. Or else the wine may be forced at high pressure through filters. One way or another, the wine is clarified.

Aperitifs and after-dinner wines will then be fortified with brandy or other distilled spirit.

High-quality red wines may then be aged in oak barrels for two years or more. Cheap wines and white wines are not usually aged in oak, but bottled as soon as they are clear.

Good wines will be further aged in the bottles, reds up to ten years, whites up to five years. This occupancy of valuable storage space for long periods is an important element in the cost of good wines.

A finished wine contains ethyl alcohol, sugar, pigments from the skin or juice which give it colour, half a dozen vitamins, fifteen or more minerals, a score of organic acids, and minute traces of many other substances. It is, as you see, an exceedingly complex beverage; slight variations in the proportions of the various constituents will produce noticeable differences in the flavour and bouquet of the wine.

AMATEUR METHODS

Red Wine

Now let's see how we can adapt the commercial process for home use. Here's a step-by-step method for red wine, described in general terms; in Chapter 5, there will be a number of detailed recipes.

1. Prepare your equipment. Every container and instrument must be scrupulously clean, free from leaks, and in full working order. Dirt, spillage and delays may jeopardize your chances of success.

2. Prepare the yeast starter, 3% to 5% of the volume of must you are going to make; or purchase sufficient dry wine yeast to inoculate the volume of must.

3. Prepare the must. With grapes, this involves crushing and de-stemming; other fruits may need chopping and soaking.

4. Check sugar and acid content, and adjust to the recommended proportions.

5. Sterilize the must with sulphur dioxide, 120 parts per million.

6. Add the yeast starter. Cover the fermentor to exclude flies, dust and airborne bacteria.

7. Stir twice a day for two to four days to break the cap. Check the temperature of the must each time. Warm it or cool it if necessary.

8. Draw off the raw wine and press the pulp. Place the liquid in secondary fermentors and apply fermentation locks. Keep 15% of the total apart for subsequent topping-up.

9. After three weeks, rack and top up.

10. After three months, rack again. Add sulphur dioxide, 60 parts per million. Top up.

11. After another three months, rack again. Clarify with finings if necessary. Add sulphur dioxide, 60 parts per million. Top up.

12. Age the wine in bulk at least six months, preferably a year.

13. Draw off the wine into bottles. Consume it or, if you have the will-power, keep some of it to age further in bottle.

So much, then, for our preliminary survey of wine and winemaking methods. The following chapters will show in minute detail how to carry out each step of the process.

White Wine

White wines are not usually fermented on pulp, therefore the open primary fermentor can be eliminated, especially when using grapes. White wines are very subject to oxidation, hence the procedure differs in some respects from that for red wines. Here are the steps:

1. Same as for red wine.

2. Same as for red wine.

3. Crush, sulphite to 120 parts per million, press out juice into secondary fermentor. Don't fill it more than three-quarters full.

4. Same as for red wine.

5. Allow to settle 8-12 hours in a cool place. Rack to remove settled solids.

6. Same as for red wine.

7. Check temperature daily; warm or cool if necessary.

8. Rack and top up when 60% of sugar has been converted. Attach fermentation locks.

9. After another 14-21 days rack and top up again; avoid aerating.

10. After 3 months wine should be clear; if not, add finings.

11. Wine, now 4-5 months old, should be bright and stable. Sulphite to 60 parts per million and bottle. Age another 6 months in cool, dark place.

CONCLUSION

Familiarize yourself with commercial wines; taste as many of them as you can, to discover what kinds you prefer. Then, using sound, scientific techniques, direct your own wine production accordingly.

2. Equipment for the Winemaker

One advantage of winemaking as a hobby is that you can start, in a small way, without spending a cent for equipment, using various utensils that you already have about the house. On the other hand, the serious amateur winemaker can go on forever improving his equipment in order to make wine more enjoyably and more efficiently.

Winemakers can be divided into three groups:

1. The small-scale winemaker who occasionally makes a gallon or two of wine out of some surplus garden fruit, or from wild fruits, flowers and herbs.

2. The medium-scale winemaker who fairly regularly produces wine in five-gallon batches, often using bought materials such as fruit concentrates.

3. The large-scale winemaker, the dedicated amateur, who makes forty gallons or more at a time from wine grapes.

One point deserves to be stressed right at the start: *cleanliness* is the key to successful winemaking. Every piece of equipment—siphon tube, funnel, thermometer, bottles, or what have you—must be scrupulously clean before it is used; it should be washed and dried after use; it should be stored in some place where as little dust as possible can settle on it.

Slackness on this point will sooner or later lead to spoilage of your wine. Careful attention to it will ensure that you get the best possible results from your ingredients and apparatus.

A two-gallon polythene pail will serve very well to contain the primary fermentation for small-scale winemaking.

A few people distrust plastic material for wine containers, claiming it imparts a bad flavour to the wine. This may have been true when plastic vessels first came on the market, but it is not true now. Countless thousands of plastic fermenting vessels and storage bottles are now in use and very few of them have caused complaints from the users. Some of the complainants, moreover, have undoubtedly produced the bad flavours by using inferior ingredients or by careless processing of the wine.

Plastic vessels are light; they are not fragile like glass; they cannot, like oak cooperage, become permanently contaminated by harmful bacteria; they are cheap.

Pails or other containers should be bought without lids. The lid is either too tight and won't let gas escape, or it's too loose and lets flies get in. The lidded containers also cost more than the lidless.

The so-called stone crock—actually glazed earthenware—makes a good primary fermentor. It is cylindrical in shape, open at the top. You can buy these crocks at some kitchenware stores or look for them in junk stores. They come in several sizes. The two-gallon size will hold one gallon of fermenting must. Note that a primary fermentor must have lots of spare capacity to prevent the foam from running over the rim. In buying second-hand crocks, be sure that the glaze has no cracks or chipped places. The stone crock has only two disadvantages: it is heavy and it is breakable.

A two-gallon stainless-steel preserving pan will serve your purpose. So will an enamelled pan, provided the enamel is sound. A chipped spot that lets the must reach the iron body of the pan will ruin the taste of your wine.

The safe rule is never to let any metal other than stainless steel come in contact with your wine.

For five-gallon batches of wine the handiest fermentor is a plastic tub or pail of at least seven gallons capacity, available at hardware stores. Or a ten-gallon stone crock will do, so long as you're not going to move it about. Remember that a crock of this size, two-thirds full of must, is heavy enough to put a crick in your backbone.

A plastic trash pail of ten to twenty gallons capacity (Fig. 1) does very well for somewhat larger batches.

Fig. 1. Primary fermentor—plastic trash pail, 10-20 gals., on 2'-high bench.

For a forty-gallon batch you will need one open-ended sixty-gallon oak barrel or two or more smaller open-ended barrels with a total capacity of at least sixty gallons. Or you can use fir barrels, waxed inside.

You can buy two kinds of large-capacity plastic containers. One is a heavy-duty plastic bag, about 6 to 8 mils thick, and 6 feet long by 4 feet wide. This can be fitted inside any container that will keep it rigid, for example a steel drum, or an old, leaky wooden barrel. It costs only about a dollar, so is cheap enough to use once and throw away, if you choose to avoid the trouble of cleaning it.

There are also semi-rigid plastic drum liners, about 1/16 to 1/8 inch thick. They are stiff enough to stand on their own when filled with grape must. They are easy to clean and, with moderate care, will last for years. They cost $15 to $20.

COVERS

The best cover for primary fermentors of all sizes is a piece of sheet plastic, held down tight with string or elastic bands.

GRAPE CRUSHERS

Some people think that the crusher is the same as the press. They are entirely different machines, for different purposes. The crusher does not compress the grapes, but is used to break the skins and let the juice run out.

The crusher is a funnel-shaped metal or wooden hopper containing one or two hand-cranked or power-driven toothed rollers. The single-roller type is preferable.

For the large-scale winemaker, a crusher is a good investment at $50 to $60. You can de-stem your grapes before crushing them, or place a heavy 1 to 1-1/2-inch wire mesh under the discharge vent of the crusher to catch the stems while the grapes fall through into the primary fermentor (Fig. 2).

Fig. 2. Crusher, with wire mesh to catch stems.

Some grape merchants will rent you a crusher, but unless these rental machines are properly cleaned and sterilized, they could become a serious source of contamination.

DE-STEMMER

If you have not de-stemmed the grapes before crushing, here's a handy gadget to pull stems and leaves out of the must. Hammer a handful of three-inch nails through a board (Fig. 3). Use it like a rake: dip it into the must and pull it out again, holding it on a slant, with the nail-points upward. It will catch the stems and leaves as they float in the must.

Fig. 3. De-stemmer.

PRESS

For pressing out grape-juice to make white wine, or for pressing the residual juice from the pulp after the primary fermentation of red wine, you need some kind of a press. The press has three main parts: a basket-like container to hold the pulp, usually made of strong wooden slats held together by metal hoops; a screw-driven plunger which by way of the plate exerts pressure on the pulp; a tray to collect the expressed juice. Presses are rated by the capacity of crushed grapes they will handle at one pressing. (See Figs. 4 and 5.)

Here are some hints on the operation of the press:

1. Note that, for white wine, pressing immediately follows crushing, but for red wine pressing is delayed until after the primary fermentation, during which the alcohol has extracted colour and flavour from the grape skins. In both cases the free-run wine or must is siphoned off first.

2. Pack the press basket, making sure the fruit is level at the top. Place the plate on top of the fruit.

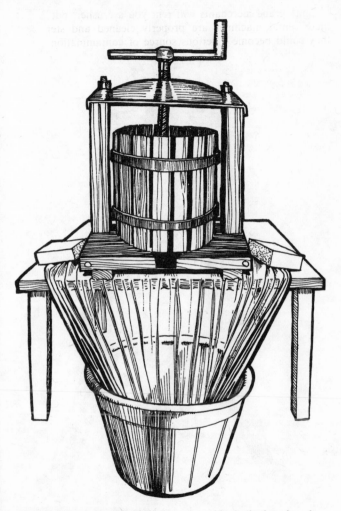

Fig. 4. Miniature press, 50 lbs. capacity, with plastic-sheet funnel.

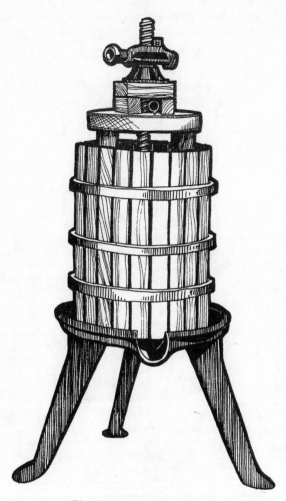

Fig. 5. Press, 500 lbs. capacity.

3. Apply pressure *slowly,* until you feel a fair resistance, then wait five or ten minutes while juice runs out the bottom of the press.

4. Screw down a little further and wait again while the juice runs out.

5. Repeat the tightening and waiting until no more juice is obtained.

6. Raise the screw, lift off the plate and remove the dry pulp.

Warning: On no account try to speed the process by screwing the press all the way down at once. You are likely to damage the press, and you will get a smaller yield of juice.

A press is not necessary for making red wine. After the first fermentation siphon off the free-run wine, then make one or two runs of "false wine" and finally throw away the pulp or "marc," sacrificing three or four gallons of the second- or third-run wine to save the time, effort and investment of pressing.

Pressing will be necessary, though, for making white wines.

SIPHON

Siphoning, or racking, is the easiest and safest way to transfer wine from one vessel to another. (Ever try pouring from a ten-gallon crock into a bottle? Ladling with a jug is messy and wasteful, and risks contaminating your wine.) For small-scale production a five-foot length of rubber tube, 1/4-inch interior diameter, will be enough. You can buy this at a drug store.

Transparent plastic tube of the same dimensions will serve for a siphon, too. Some winemakers prefer plastic because they can see the wine going through it. But all the plastic tubing I have seen has a certain amount of spring to it; it tends to return to the coiled shape in which it left the factory. It is therefore not so easy to manipulate as a rubber tube, which will hang straight and stay where you put it.

Seven feet of quarter-inch tubing is needed for medium-scale production.

For large-scale winemaking this tubing is too small to move

the wine fast enough. Instead, get nine feet of plastic garden hose, of half-inch internal diameter. (In this size the plastic pipe is more flexible and manageable than the corresponding rubber hose.)

Fig. 6. Pump-siphon.

SECONDARY FERMENTORS

For small-scale wine making a few one-gallon jugs will contain your wine during the secondary, slow fermentation, after it has been taken off the pulp. If you have none on hand, you can get them cheaply at a junk store. Nothing smaller should be used, since the more you mess the wine about, siphoning or pouring it into small bottles, the greater the risk of contamination. Moreover, the smaller the bottle, the more rapid and extreme will be fluctuations of temperature in response to changes in the air temperature. Your containers, whether one-gallon jugs or something else of similar size, must have narrow necks, to permit the fitting of fermentation locks (Fig. 7).

Five-gallon plastic carboys are best for medium-scale wine-making. Glass carboys are good, but are heavy and fragile. For larger operations, oak barrels are best, but they need a certain amount of care (see Chapter 6). Therefore many winemakers use instead a number of five-gallon or ten-gallon plastic or glass carboys.

STRAINERS

Racking will remove the heavier waste material from your wine, but a strainer is handy to catch grape-seeds and such floating particles, on the first racking from the primary fermentor.

A plastic strainer mounted in a funnel (Fig. 8) is best. Stainless steel mesh is good, too. Or you can strain through

Fig. 7. Secondary fermentation vessel—10-gal. plastic carboy, with fermentation lock in place.

Fig. 8. Top: Strainer. Bottom: Plastic funnel with inter-changeable filter.

open-weave nylon fabric such as lingerie, or men's nylon shirts. An open-weave cotton cloth is good, too.

But *don't* try to filter your wine. The only safe method is with a closed pressure-filtration system such as the commercial wineries use, and few amateurs want so much trouble and expense. Open filtration exposes the wine excessively to the air. It's needless, anyway; racking and fining will give you crystal-clear wine, safely.

FUNNELS

For making a few bottles of wine, you can get by without a funnel. Medium and large-scale bottling operations will be easier if you use one. If you are bottling from the spigot of a barrel, a funnel is essential. Funnels are also useful for blending small quantities of wine or for adding sugar syrup to bottles or fermentors.

I recommend plastic funnels. The important dimension on a funnel is the size of the spout or tip. Make sure it is small enough to enter the opening of the bottle or container you want to fill.

Different manufacturers have different methods of describing the sizes of their funnels. Some refer to the number of fluid ounces held by the conical or cup-shaped upper part of the funnel. Using this scale, 8 oz. to 16 oz. funnels would be about right for filling 26 oz. bottles; 24-32 oz. for gallon jugs, and 64-128 oz. for large demijohns or barrels.

FERMENTATION LOCKS

So long as your wine is fermenting, it is giving off carbon dioxide gas. This gas production is obvious during the early stages of the process; you can hear a steady hissing from the fermentor and, if it is of glass, you can see bubbles rising through the liquid. The gas must escape, or it will build up pressure which can blow corks and make a mess in your winery. Worse, the pressure can burst a bottle, and the flying glass can disfigure or blind you.

To be sure, gas pressure gives the characteristic effervescence to Champagne and other sparkling wines, but such wines are made by a rigorously controlled process and then stored in special, pressure-resistant bottles (see Chapter 9). For the present, let's take it as a general rule that we let the carbon dioxide escape from fermenting wine.

Simply to leave the vessels open would let the gas out, but it would let in air, whose oxygen would combine with certain ingredients of the wine and impair its colour and flavour. Moreover an open bottle-neck would admit vinegar bacteria. These bacteria float freely in the atmosphere and some of them, sooner or later, will reach and contaminate any wine which is left exposed. Aiding the spread of the bacteria is a tiny fly which swarms around and feeds upon fruits and fruit-juices. Exposed wine will attract these pests, whose feet may be laden with bacteria from the rotting apples in your neighbour's garbage can. Then you can say, "Goodbye, wine! Hello, vinegar!"

The fermentation lock (Fig. 9) is a low-pressure valve mounted on a short piece of plastic tube. The tube passes through a pierced rubber bung (better than a cork for this purpose) which is placed in the mouth of the fermentor. Inside the fermentation lock is a small cavity or well, containing some metabisulphite solution. Empty the lock and refill with fresh solution every six weeks.

Here's how it works. So long as carbon dioxide is being produced it must bubble through the metabisulphite solution in order to escape. But when fermentation stops, air cannot

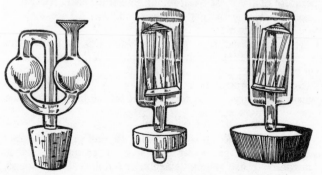

Fig. 9. Two types of fermentation locks, with 3 types of stoppers.

get in. The lock also forms a positive barrier to spoilage bacteria and fruit flies.

There are many models of fermentation locks, and for efficiency there is little to choose between them. The glass locks, however, are fragile; the least roughness when inserting or removing them, or an accidental knock with the elbow, will break them. Therefore I recommend plastic locks. You will, of course, need one lock for each secondary fermentor.

The trifling cost of a few fermentation locks and a little metabisulphite is good insurance against the loss of ingredients and labour, and the acute annoyance, when a batch of promising wine turns to vinegar.

VINOMETER

The vinometer (Fig. 10) is a small instrument that measures the alcohol content of a finished wine. It is accurate to within one percent for dry wines, but is inaccurate for sweet wines. Instructions for use come with the instrument.

THERMOMETERS

For rapid, reliable winemaking, you should know the temperature of your must. Immersion thermometers (Fig. 11) are handy. They float in the must and let you check its temperature at any time.

In a large primary fermentor, you can reduce the temperature of the must by dropping into it a plastic bag full of cracked ice. Tie the bag tightly so that, as the ice melts, it won't dilute the must.

If the temperature of the must is too low, you can place an electric heating pad under a primary fermentor, or tie it on to the side of a secondary fermentor.

Suitable fermentation temperatures will be mentioned, where necessary, in the recipes that follow in Chapter 5.

BOILER

If you need to boil your water to remove hardness or expel chlorine, get a big stock-pot or preserving-pan, at least three to five gallons capacity, of stainless steel or sound, uncracked enamel.

Fig. 10. Vinometer.   Fig. 11. Thermometer.

STIRRER

A wooden kitchen spoon is the best thing for stirring the fermenting must and breaking the cap. A clean stick makes a fair substitute.

PUMP

If you are making 50 gallons of wine or more at a time, I recommend the use of a pump. A small plastic impeller pump (Fig. 12), capable of moving 3 to 5 gallons a minute, will cost $18 to $22. The pump and a 1/4-h.p. motor to drive it can be mounted on a plywood base. The whole outfit, including 30 feet of clear plastic hose, 1/2 inch interior diameter, should not cost more than $50 for a do-it-yourselfer, and it's worth every cent. It can be the most

Fig. 12. Pump, with electric motor.

useful piece of equipment in the wine cellar of any large-scale winemaker.

CIDER AND PERRY EQUIPMENT

Grape crushers and presses are no good for use with apples and pears. The special equipment for processing these fruits has not been made for the past twenty years, so has only been available second-hand. But the demand for it is growing, and manufacturers are becoming interested. We may soon see new, improved apple and pear crushers and presses on the market.

METABISULPHITE AND OTHER STERILANTS

You can, if you wish, make up a solution of Campden tablets (1 tablet to 4 ounces water) for filling fermentation locks and sterilizing equipment. but it is cheaper to buy potassium or sodium metabisulphite crystals at your wine-makers' supply store. Dissolve 2 ounces of metabisulphite in one gallon of water and keep it in a tightly stoppered bottle. This will last the average winemaker six months for filling fermentation locks and general sterilizing purposes.

For cleaning bottles and equipment, you can use chlorin-

24

ated detergent, available at the supply store. *Do not use household chlorine bleaches.* Chlorine kills all spoilage organisms, but it also kills wine yeast, so be sure that all equipment cleaned with this detergent is thoroughly rinsed before you put must into it. *Do not use chlorinated detergent in barrels.* For cleaning and sterilizing barrels, see the instructions in Chapter 6.

Very effective as bactericides—although not as cleaners— are quaternary ammonium compounds. Usually diluted to two parts per thousand in warm water, they will sterilize any kind of winemaking equipment, including barrels. Carefully follow the directions that come with these compounds, for actual use and for the subsequent rinsing of equipment.

CONCLUSION

You don't need a lot of equipment to start winemaking. In any case, elaborate equipment is no substitute for the winemaker's personal care and patience. Most successful winemakers start out modestly, and gradually enlarge the scale of their operations.

3. Ingredients

As mentioned in Chapter 1, you can make wine out of almost any kind of fruit. But there are some other things, beside the fruit base, that you'll need. So let's talk about the various wine ingredients, with some suggestions on their relative merits, and some hints on where to get them and how best to handle them.

GRAPES

The original wine grape, cultivated for thousands of years in Europe, and now flourishing in California, is called *Vitis vinifera*. There are more than five thousand *vinifera* varieties, adapted to various combinations of soil and climate, and yielding widely different types of wine.

California Grapes

The California *vinifera* grapes usually become available about September 10, and continue on the market till about October 1.

The most common variety is Zinfandel. Zinfandel is a red or blue grape with white juice, so it will make white wine if you press and ferment the juice alone, or red wine if you ferment on the skins and let the alcohol extract the pigment.

Zinfandels grown in the cooler regions of California, such as the area around San Francisco, make the best wine, but all of these go to the commercial wineries. Amateur winemakers are left with the grapes grown in the central valleys where the climate is a little too hot to produce first-class grapes for table wine. Unfortunately the same thing applies to most of the California grapes available to amateurs.

The Alicante grape has red juice as well as a red skin, so it will make only red wine, one which is very aromatic and heavy. I recommend that it be used only in a blend, to add colour to a wine based on some other grape.

The Mission grape has red skin and white juice; it does not make very good wine alone. Here, too, it should be used as a blending grape for sugar content or colour.

Grenache, in our opinion, makes a very good wine, but it is seldom available.

Some grape growers are now becoming aware of the increasing demand from amateurs for high-quality grape varieties, and are realizing that they can get a better price by selling direct to amateurs. For instance, the price of Cabernet Sauvignon—a superb wine grape—is two or three times that of Zinfandels, but the devoted amateur will gladly pay it. Consult your winemakers' supply store for sources of fancy grape varieties.

As for white grapes, the only ones generally available so far have been Muscatel, Thompson Seedless and Palominos. The Muscatel, as it is grown in California, does not make good table wine. It usually comes from the hot areas, and has a high sugar content and a very strong muscat flavour. In California, Muscatel is usually made into a sweet, fortified wine, rather than a table wine.

In view of the fact that white table wine is more delicate, and consequently more difficult to make, than red wine, I suggest that you wait until you are an accomplished winemaker before attempting it. Then the best method is to use a blend of grapes, excluding the Muscatel.

Riesling, Chardonnay, Alligoté and Sylvaner are all excellent white grapes, but are difficult to obtain because of the demand by the wineries. Still, there's no harm in trying.

If all else fails, you could use the Thompson Seedless. It is really a table grape and, if used alone, makes a rather tasteless wine. But it can be improved somewhat by the addition of some acid and a little tannin.

To buy California grapes, ask among the fruit importers or wholesalers of your area. You will usually find several of them clustered in one district. Don't wait till September to make these inquiries; see the merchant in early summer and have him phone you as soon as the grapes arrive.

Don't buy the cheapest! This is a poor place to save money. Get the best available, remembering that an extra cent a pound makes very little difference to the cost of the finished wine. Look for firm grapes, free from mould. Avoid raisined grapes, which are overripe.

The most common error among winemakers is to seek out the sweetest grapes. The wholesaler will probably tell you that his grapes are wonderful because they contain 28% sugar. He may even stretch the truth a little, because he knows most of his customers are impressed by a high sugar content.

But there's no need to scramble for the sweetest grapes. Almost all the California varieties are sweet enough for making table wine; indeed, most of them are too sweet. You don't want more than 12% or 13% alcohol by volume in your finished wine, so the best grapes for your purpose will have a Balling of about 23% to 24% (Balling is a scale that indicates the percentage of sugar in the juice) or a specific gravity of 1.090 to 1.100. (For an explanation of specific gravity, see Chapter 4.)

Take your hydrometer with you when you shop for grapes. The wholesaler will probably let you squeeze enough grapes to fill your testing jar and take a reading on the spot. Remember that, since this fresh juice contains some suspended solids, you should deduct 1.6% Balling or 7 degrees S.G. from the apparent reading to get a true value for the sugar content.

What quantity of grapes should you buy?

First, consider how much wine you want. The juice yield of the grapes varies somewhat from year to year, but you can estimate that sixteen pounds of grapes, allowing for losses in processing, will give you one gallon of finished wine. The grapes usually come in boxes, each containing 30 to 34 pounds, so each box will make about two gallons.

Second, consider the capacity of your primary fermentor. You can't fill it right up with must, since you have to allow at least one-fifth of its capacity for expansion during the primary fermentation. With this allowance, a barrel of 50 gallons capacity will handle about 400 pounds of grapes (12 boxes) and will yield about 25 gallons of finished first-run wine.

The wholesaler will deliver the grapes to your premises. Have your grape-crusher and fermentor set up and ready for use, where the delivery men can crush the grapes straight into the fermentor. They will usually do this free of charge if you buy ten boxes or more.

So much for buying your California grapes. We shall see in later chapters how to continue with making the wine.

American Grapes

All *vinifera* grapes spring from imported European stocks. But there were also grapes growing on this continent before the white man arrived. Some of these native grapes have been greatly improved by plant breeders.

Vitis labrusca, the Northern Fox Grape, is the ancestor of Isabella, Catawba, Delaware and other cultivated varieties including the Concord, probably the best-known, because it is so widely eaten as a table grape, and is used to make huge quantities of canned and bottled grape-juice. *Labruscas* will stand much colder winters than will any *vinifera*. They grow well throughout the North-eastern United States and in parts of Canada.

Labruscas all have more or less of the special "foxy" flavour derived from their wild ancestor. Some people are fond of foxy grapes and wine, others find the flavour unpleasant. If you enjoy eating Concord grapes, you should certainly try a batch of *labrusca* wine.

Most northern-grown *labruscas*, by the way, are very high in acid and low in sugar compared with the California *viniferas*. We'll see in Chapter 4 how to measure acid and

29

sugar and how to correct deficiencies and excesses. Many *labruscas* also contain a lot of pectin—good for making jelly, but a disadvantage for wine. That, too, can be corrected.

Another important native American grape is *Vitis rotundifolia*, which prefers a warmer climate than *labrusca*. There are selected, improved varieties of *rotundifolia*, too, such as Scuppernong and Muscadine.

The advantage of the native American grapes is that because they are so widely grown, you can buy them anywhere without much trouble.

Concords, for example, are usually available at your supermarket in September. They are more expensive than *viniferas*, but I treat them, as you'll see later, like a tree-fruit, using just enough to give flavour and colour to the wine. Wine from American grapes, therefore, usually costs less per gallon than that from *viniferas*. The best place to look for them is your neighbour's back yard.

Hybrid Grapes

The hybrids are crosses between *viniferas* and native varieties. They combine the qualities of both parents—the flavour of the *vinifera* and the hardiness of the native grape. They also tend to be more productive than the *viniferas*. Some hybrids have the *labrusca* foxy taste, others don't.

Hybrids are usually named after the grower who developed them. I was very impressed with wine from Seibel #9549, and Seibel #10878 is widely grown and recommended in Eastern U.S.A. Another man who produced well-known hybrids is Maurice Baco, whose Baco #1 is well recommended.

Consult your state department of agricultural information about the best non-foxy hybrids grown in your area.

Grown in the relatively cool climates of the North-Eastern and North-Western U.S.A. and of Eastern and Western Canada, hybrids naturally don't have the high sugar content of the California *viniferas*. Still, in good years, they will produce 18% to 22% sugar. You will have to add extra sugar to get a good table wine from the northern hybrids.

Home-Grown Grapes

You may already have a grape-vine in your garden. If so, try a batch of wine from its fruit. If you have no vines, why not get one? To be sure, there are some areas where grapes simply won't grow. But don't give up too easily; there are some amazingly hardy varieties now available.

Don't buy grape-vines by mail from a firm half-way across the continent. Ask around the neighbourhood; go to your nearest nurseryman; find a local gardening club; seek out your government horticultural information service. In other words, get expert local advice and select a grape that will do well in your soil and your climate.

Any good gardening book will tell you how to plant, cultivate and prune your vine. Its lush foliage, trained up a fence or trellis, is an ornament to your garden. Then, when the grapes come along, you enjoy the ultimate satisfaction of having the entire winemaking process under your own control, right from the soil to the bottle. And don't forget the economics of it. You'll have some exceedingly inexpensive wine!

Blending Grapes

Probably the best red table wine you can make will come from blending a hybrid with a California *vinifera* grape. The former is low in sugar, high in acid; the latter, low in acid, high in sugar. The resultant blend has the ideal sugar and acid content without the addition of any tartaric acid, sugar or water.

A fifty-fifty blend, or 60% hybrid with 40% *vinifera,* can make an exceptional wine. Some people use as little as 10% of the California grape and they feel the resultant light, fresh-tasting wine is superb.

Once you get some experience in winemaking and begin blending, your own taste will be your guide. One of the pleasures of winemaking is that it offers limitless scope for experiment.

FRUIT CONCENTRATES

Fruit concentrates have long been available to the food

industry, but many of them were not suitable for winemaking because they contained yeast inhibitors, or were carmelized by excessive heating. Grape concentrates, too, have been made for years in Spain, Portugal, Algeria, Italy, France, Cyprus and California, but these were not available to amateurs. They were used to improve musts of low sugar content in seasons when cool weather had prevented the grape harvest from ripening properly.

But now a whole new world has opened up to amateur winemakers with the advent of concentrated fruit that is free from preservatives or added sugar. You can make excellent wine from concentrates alone, or you can combine concentrates with fresh fruit.

Grape concentrate is far the most popular, just as grapes are the most popular fruit for winemaking. But the amateur is missing a lot if he overlooks the other concentrates such as apricot, peach, apple and fig, to mention just a few.

Here are the advantages of concentrates for winemakers:

1. The fruit is tree-ripened, instead of being picked prematurely in order to stand up to shipment.

2. There is very little pulp to strain out of the must.

3. The concentrate is pasteurized and therefore is free from wild yeasts and spoilage organisms.

4. There is much less work involved than in making wine from fresh fruit.

5. You can usually make wine more cheaply with concentrate than with imported fruit, because you avoid paying freight on all the water that was removed prior to the canning or bottling.

Are you interested? Then let's see how these useful concentrates are made.

The fruit is crushed and pressed, then the juice is dehydrated in vacuum, either with or without application of heat. The cold process produces better results for our purpose, but hot-pressed concentrates are fine, provided the heat is not so high as to produce carmelization of the sugar content.

The degree of concentration varies from two-to-one to ten-to-one, depending on the fruit involved. You can appreciate that, with the high original sugar content of grapes, a four-to-one concentrate is almost solid sugar. Apple juice, with a lower initial sugar content, will stand eight-to-one or nine-to-one concentration.

Grape Concentrates

Grape concentrate, at first sight, seems the most expensive, but if you consider how much sugar you are getting, you'll see that it's not necessarily more expensive than others. The best grape concentrates I have found so far come from Spain, California and Cyprus, in that order.

The Spanish is the most concentrated. It usually has a specific gravity of 1.390 and is almost solid when you open the can. It also seems to have the best colour, particularly the red or Tintorero, as they call it. It comes packed in three-quart cans. One can of concentrate is equivalent to almost 65 pounds of fresh grapes.

This can of concentrate has been selling for about seven or eight dollars, and when you can buy grapes that someone else has grown, picked, crushed, pressed, strained and pasteurized at that price, in my opinion it's a good buy.

How much wine will this concentrate yield? It normally takes about sixteen pounds of grapes to make one gallon of wine, so this can of concentrate, when diluted with water and fermented, will give you four gallons (twenty-four bottles) of good table wine, with little or no sugar added. That works out at about 30 to 33 cents a bottle. Compare that with the price of the equivalent imported wine at your liquor store!

You can, if you wish, add sugar and so get increased alcohol content and some residual sweetness. Or you can dilute more than four-to-one (adding sugar to compensate, of course) and get a larger volume of wine. This wine will tend to be thin in body and pale in colour, but tastes vary, and many people prefer a thin wine that is not too satiating. See Chapter 5 for detailed recipes.

American grape concentrate producers have now become aware of the existence of a large market among amateurs, and are upgrading their product to meet this demand. We should expect to get some top-quality grape concentrate from this source in the near future.

Other Concentrates

Concentrated apple juice sells for about five to six dollars per 3-quart can. Diluted, it gives you apple juice for close to 60 cents a gallon. It doesn't make better cider than fresh apples, but it's so close that most people are fully satisfied with the product, and you save the work and equipment needed to extract juice from fresh apples.

Other concentrates are coming on the market almost every month, so you are sure to find one or two that suit your taste.

In Chapter 5 are recipes and detailed instructions that will start you on this highly enjoyable branch of the winemaker's art.

ACID

Good acid balance is important in winemaking. Grapes grown under ideal conditions will contain acids in the right proportion to produce good wine. The most important acids in grapes are tartaric, citric, and malic. When it is necessary to increase the acid of a must, a mixture of these three acids will give the best results.

It is vital to measure and adjust acid before fermentation commences. Full instructions are given in Chapter 4.

GRAPE TANNIN

Grape tannin is found in the skins, seeds and stems of grapes. It gives a wine astringency or character. It helps a wine clear and prolongs the life of a good wine.

Red *vinifera* grapes usually contain enough tannin. Occasionally white grapes or other fruits will lack adequate tannin and therefore it should be added. Tannin is obtainable from tea or chemically as tannic acid; but for best results, use only grape tannin.

CAMPDEN TABLETS

A Campden tablet contains about 7 grains of potassium

metabisulphite. Dissolved in a slightly acid solution such as grape juice, it releases approximately 4 grains of sulphur dioxide (SO_2). One tablet dissolved in one gallon gives 60 parts per million of SO_2.

At this concentration, few people can taste or smell the SO_2, yet it is an effective sterilizing agent. It inhibits the growth of the wild yeasts and spoilage organisms which lie on the raw fruit and float in the air, but it does not destroy cultured wine yeasts. So it gives you a completely controlled fermentation.

Moreover, Campden tablets slightly increase the acidity of the must which, in most cases, is beneficial.

Campden tablets are also added to wine before bottling, at the rate of not more than one to the gallon. At this stage the SO_2 acts as an anti-oxidant, preserves the colour of your wine, guards against bitterness and encourages the development of esters which give the wine a smooth flavour as it matures.

Crush the tablets before mixing with must or wine.

ANTIOXIDANT TABLETS OR CRYSTALS

Pure ascorbic acid added to wine at time of bottling prevents excess oxidation. One tablet contains 100 milligrams of ascorbic acid—sufficient for 1 gallon of wine. If treating large volumes of wine, crystals are more economical. Use 1 teaspoon per 6 gallons of wine.

YEAST

Many people think that yeast is an inorganic chemical like common salt, and that you simply add so many spoonfuls or ounces of it to your other ingredients, according to the kind of wine you want.

In fact, yeast is a living organism, an egg-shaped, single-celled fungus which reproduces by budding. The bud separates from the parent cell, and in two and a half hours is mature and ready in its turn to bud and divide. You can watch the process by examining a drop of fermenting must under a 100-power microscope.

As winemakers, we are not particularly interested in the

35

amount of yeast produced; indeed, we go to some trouble to remove it from the finished beverage. What we want is one of the by-products of the growth process. Yeast feeds on sugar, vitamins, minerals and water, producing roughly equal parts by weight of carbon dioxide and alcohol. We let the carbon dioxide escape and do our best to keep the alcohol.

For the best results in winemaking, the yeast should have a "friendly" or suitable environment, with the right nutrients and the right temperature. If chilled below 40°F. yeast remains dormant. The best working temperature for most wine yeasts is 65° to 75°F. Cooler ferments produce softer wines and achieve more efficient conversion of available sugars to alcohol. Hot ferments—over 80°F.—make bitter wine. Temperatures above 85°F. seriously weaken the fermenting power of any yeast, and at 95°F. or over, the yeast is killed. Some books recommend starting fermentation with a must at blood-heat, i.e. 98.6°F. This is far too high for safety. Ignore any such instructions, no matter where you read or hear them.

Yeast makes quite as important a contribution to the quality of the wine as do the other ingredients. Yeast affects flavour, aroma, clarity, strength and keeping quality.

To be sure, some people do make beverages with baker's yeast, or they depend on the wild yeasts that infest the skins of grapes and other fresh fruits. But you will get stronger, better-looking, nicer-tasting wines if you use the special yeasts that have been bred for the job. In the recipes that follow, I recommend the best kinds of yeast to use. You can buy named, tested varieties of yeast at your winemakers' supply store. You should not try to save pennies by using inferior yeasts, and so jeopardize the success of your whole winemaking operation.

Making Yeast Starters

Because yeast so readily reproduces itself, you don't have to buy much of it. Usually the selected wine yeasts are sold a fraction of an ounce in each package, but this small amount would take a long time to start any large quantity of wine fermenting. So you make what is called a "starter."

When yeast is put into the must, its development takes place in two stages. First the yeast multiplies until it has reached the optimum concentration for its environment. During this time, known as the "lag period," it is producing little or no alcohol. When the lag period is over, then begins the heavy fermentation, with hissing and foaming as the carbon dioxide bubbles off, and with rapid formation of alcohol.

The longer the lag period, the greater the risk that spoilage organisms will get established in the must. The way to shorten the lag period is to begin with a lot of yeast. That's why you need a starter. For best results, this starter should be about 3% to 5% of the total volume of must.

Say you want a starter for five gallons of wine. Get a clean 40-ounce bottle or jar. Make a solution of "yeast starter," obtainable from any winemakers' supply store, and add your yeast culture. Cover the jar with sheet plastic, well tied down, or plug the bottle-neck with cotton batting. Keep the starter at 60° to 70°F. and in a day or two you should see signs of life in the form of bubbles rising through the liquid. It is then ready for use.

Forty ounces is about right for five gallons of must. For bigger brews, use bigger starters. Never skimp on your starter. You can't have too much yeast to start with; the commonest error is to have too little. You need not fear getting a "yeasty" taste in your wine; that comes, not from using a strong starter, but from using the wrong kind of yeast, from failure to rack properly, or from drinking the beverage too new.

A wine yeast is now produced that does not require the preparation of a starter. It is packaged in foil envelopes containing 5 grams; each is sufficient to start 5 gallons of must. This product keeps indefinitely at room temperature. It is a Burgundy strain, suitable as an all-purpose wine yeast, and is very economical. The trade name is Andovin.

Preserving Yeast

There's no need to buy fresh cultured yeast every time you brew wine. Here's how to save yeast from one batch to the next batch of the same kind.

Don't try to save any of the heavy sediment at the bottom of the primary fermentor, which contains a lot of vegetable matter that would decay. But after racking off from the secondary fermentor you will have a fairly pure sediment of yeast left at the bottom. Pour or ladle this yeast into a bottle (preferably a brown one to exclude light), cap it tightly and keep it in your refrigerator at about 40°F. (Don't freeze it!)

Some wine yeasts will keep for months under refrigeration. But be careful when you take the yeast out. *Don't* let it come to room temperature before opening the bottle, or there may be a dangerous build-up of pressure.

YEAST NUTRIENT

Yeast, like a child, will grow best if properly nourished. If undernourished, it may not die at once, but it cannot give of its best in alcohol production or in flavour. Many of the fruits from which we make wine are to some degree lacking in the elements which wine yeast needs if it is to thrive. So we add a nutrient containing salts that produce nitrogen. This invigorates the yeast and helps it to make best use of the sugar and other ingredients in the must; it tends to make the wine stronger, clearer, and ready to drink sooner.

Proprietary brands of yeast nutrient are available, and each package bears instructions for use. Nutrients will not usually be needed in wines made from pure, fresh grape juice. In recipes for other wines, the quantities of nutrient required will be indicated.

YEAST INHIBITOR

There is no satisfactory product available to amateurs that will stop an actively fermenting must. I do not suggest you attempt to halt fermentation except by pasteurization.

Potassium sorbate, by preventing yeast from budding, will inhibit renewed fermentation in a clear, stable wine. It will *not* stop active fermentation.

SUGAR

Only grapes—and not all varieties of these—contain

enough sugar to make first-class, strong wine. Many wines, then, require the addition of more or less sugar. Extra sugar is also used for sweetening a dry wine, for producing the effervescence in a sparkling wine, and for other purposes.

Often the most convenient way to add sugar is in the form of syrup. You can make a supply of standard syrup by dissolving 6 lbs. of sugar in 4 pints of water. This will make one gallon of syrup, with a specific gravity of 1.300. Pasteurize by boiling, and keep tightly capped.

WATER

For many wine recipes you have to use water, and of course the final flavour will be altered if your water has some kind of flavour to begin with, particularly in light-tasting beverages such as white wines.

If your water is heavily chlorinated (more than 5 parts per million) you should boil it. Boiling drives off most of the chlorine and, with hard water, precipitates some of the dissolved minerals.

COLOURS

Artificial colours, and colours extracted from grape-skins, are available to amateurs. Most wine-producing countries restrict the use of colour by commercial wineries, but naturally the amateur is free to use it. Use only proper wine colour, obtained from a specialty store. Bakery colours from the grocer may not tolerate the acids and other ingredients in wine.

PECTIC ENZYMES

Most fruits contain more or less pectin, the substance which makes jams and jellies set. Pectin is a nuisance in winemaking, since it tends to hold solids in suspension, making the wine cloudy. Pectinase is an enzyme that removes pectin from the fruit. Various manufacturers put it up under brand names. Used in accordance with directions it gives you more juice from your fruit and produces a wine of richer colour, finer flavour, and crystalline clarity.

CONCLUSION

Don't skimp on ingredients, either in quantity or quality. It's false economy to cut 1% from the cost of your wine, if it means a 20% loss of quality.

Try a wide range of ingredients. Don't get into a rut with your winemaking—turn it into an adventure.

4. Sugar and Acid Control

A cabinet-maker measures the wood before he starts to build; a dressmaker measures the fabric before she starts to sew. The careful winemaker measures his ingredients before he sets them fermenting. But this measurement is not without some complications. You can measure grapes by weight or juices by volume, and still not know the composition of your must. Grapes vary widely between one variety and another; each variety varies from year to year. The same applies to all fruits.

There are two major variables in the must: sugar and acid. By appropriate tests, you can measure the proportions of sugar and acid and can, if need be, correct deficiencies or excesses.

Let's begin with sugar control. The key instrument for this purpose is the hydrometer.

HYDROMETERS AND SPECIFIC GRAVITY

The literal meaning of the word "hydrometer" is "water measurer" and its function is measuring the density of liquids. In winemaking we use it to measure the density of such things as grape-juice, fermenting wine or fruit concentrate, in relation to the density of pure water. That is, we measure the ratio between the weight of a given volume of the liquid nd the weight of the same volume of water.

This ratio is called the *specific gravity* of the liquid, usually abbreviated to S.G. (and sometimes called merely "gravity").

If the liquid has exactly the same density as water, its S.G. is 1.000 (S.G. is usually read to three decimal places). If it is denser than water, its S.G. is more than 1.000.

A hydrometer is a sealed glass tube with a weighted bulb at one end that makes it float upright in a liquid. Inside the tube is a printed paper scale. To read the hydrometer you note where the surface of the liquid in which it is floating cuts across the scale. The denser the liquid, the higher the instrument will float in it, just as a swimmer or a ship floats higher in salt water than in fresh. The less dense the liquid, the deeper the instrument sinks. So the *high* S.G. readings (over 1.000) are at the *bottom* of the scale and the *low* readings (less than 1.000) at the *top*.

A hydrometer in pure water reads 1.000. If you add sugar, the S.G. increases, because the liquid is getting denser. You can raise the S.G. to 1.100, 1.200 and so on, up to 1.400, at which point your solution is nearly solid sugar.

Suppose you have a barrel of grape-juice, S.G. 1.095, and you add yeast. As the juice ferments, its S.G. will fall, because sugar is being converted into alcohol, which is lighter than water. (The S.G. of pure alcohol is 0.792.)

So the S.G. of a dry table wine, containing little or no sugar, will be below 1.000. It is less dense than water because it is principally a mixture of alcohol and water.

Simply by using the hydrometer to measure specific gravity, you can do many things to control and improve your wine-making:

1. Measure the sugar content of your must.

2. Calculate the potential alcohol content of the must, before it begins to ferment.

3. Tell exactly how the fermentation is progressing.

4. Determine when the fermentation has finished.

5. Control the amount of pressure or sparkle you get in cider or champagne-type wines.

6. Measure the alcohol strength of the finished wine.

Surely these are reasons enough for any winemaker to buy and use a hydrometer!

Unfortunately there is much confusion of terminology in connection with hydrometers and their use. It arises because many different types of hydrometer have been made, for different specialized purposes, in different countries.

Since the instrument is so often used for measuring sugar content, it is sometimes called a saccharometer (sugar mea-surer) and is then fitted with a scale which reads sugar content directly. The saccharometer and hydrometer are basically the same instrument, and I shall consistently use the term "hydrometer."

There are six or seven different scales in use, but the two most popular in English-speaking countries are the Specific Gravity scale already mentioned, and the Balling (or Brix) scale, which gives a direct reading of sugar content in terms of percentage by weight. A much-used type of Balling hydro-meter has a scale reading from 0 to 30, 0 meaning no sugar and 30 meaning that 30% by weight of the liquid measured is fermentable sugar. (0 Balling = 1.000 S.G., 23.9 Balling = 1.100 S.G.)

Most winemaking books and magazines published in Eng-land use the S.G. scale; most American material uses the Balling scale. A complete conversion table for the two scales is given at the back of the book so that with an S.G. instru-ment you can quickly calculate sugar content, and with a Balling hydrometer you can calculate specific gravity. Thus you can conveniently work with recipes from any source.

Hydrometers are now being produced which contain two scales, S.G. and Balling. With one of these instruments you have instant reading of whichever figure you need.

Some printed materials quote only the digits following the decimal point of a S.G. reading. Thus a S.G. of 1.125 would be given as 125; 1.095 would be given as 95; 0.995 would become 995. The beginner should remember that. because of the unprinted unit figure and decimal point, a S.G. of 95 is *higher* than a S.G. of 995.

Though the Balling hydrometer measures percentage of sugar *by weight*, the strength of commercial alcoholic beverages is measured in percentage of alcohol *by volume*. These terms, "percentage by weight" and "percentage by volume," are two more convenient abbreviations.

There are several possible ways of expressing the components of a mixture:

Weight in weight. Suppose you have dissolved some sugar in water. The total weight of the solution is 10 lbs.; the weight of the sugar was 3 lbs. The proportion of sugar could be expressed as 30% weight in weight.

Weight in volume. In a different batch of sugar-and-water mix, you might have 2½ lbs. of sugar in one gallon of solution. The proportion of sugar is then 2½ lbs. per gallon, weight in volume.

Volume in volume. In a mixture of alcohol and water (using the metric system for a change) you might have 100 cc. alcohol in 1000 cc. of the mixture, *i.e.* 10% alcohol by volume in volume.

The terms "weight in weight" and "volume in volume" are customarily abbreviated to "X% by weight" or X% by volume."

With the ingredients used in winemaking, there will be considerable differences between the "by weight" and "by volume" proportions. For example, consider a wine which contains 12% alcohol *by weight;* the same wine has about 13.6% alcohol *by volume*. It's easy to see why winemakers, professional and amateur, like to cite figures of alcohol by volume instead of by weight—it makes the brew sound stronger!

With this explanation, you will have no difficulty reading the alcohol conversion table at the back of the book or in carrying out any of the procedures described in the book.

Winemakers often refer to the graduations on the hydrometer scale as degrees. For example: "When the S.G. of the must drops 50 degrees, siphon off the wine." This could refer to a drop from S.G. 1.095 (sometimes abbreviated as 95) to 1.045 (often written 45). Similarly the Balling scale divisions are often called degrees. This is convenient and clear, so long as you don't confuse these hydrometer "degrees" with thermometer degrees, which are often mentioned, too, in winemaking instructions.

Different brands of hydrometer have different ranges, some of them needlessly wide. For home brewing of wine, a range from .990 to 1.170 will be adequate.

USING THE HYDROMETER

It is awkward to take hydrometer readings in the vessel where your wine is fermenting. There may be a layer of floating fruit pulp—the cap—which masks the reading. The sides of the vessel stop you from looking horizontally at the scale.

For ease and accuracy the hydrometer should be floated in a clear glass or plastic cylinder. You can buy this hydrometer testing jar at the same place where you buy the hydrometer. To withdraw a sample of must or wine and transfer it without mess to the testing jar, the handiest thing is an ordinary kitchen gravy baster.

Float the hydrometer in the testing jar, then spin the instrument, by a twist of thumb and forefinger, to dislodge any air bubbles which might be clinging to its sides. These bubbles could cause serious errors.

Now, with your eye at surface level, look at the place where the hydrometer stem emerges from the liquid. Surface tension causes the liquid to climb a little way up the stem, forming a tiny curve called the "meniscus." Ignore the meniscus and see where the liquid, if it were level, would intersect the stem; that is where you should read the scale (Fig. 13).

Keep the gravy baster for this purpose alone, and carefully wash it out after each use. Scrupulous cleanliness of baster, testing jar and hydrometer will ensure that the sample is not contaminated.

Each hydrometer is calibrated to read accurately at one temperature—many at 60°F., some at 68°F. If the liquid is more than two or three degrees above or below the standard temperature, the reading will be significantly out. Consult the correction table at the back of the book to allow for this if necessary.

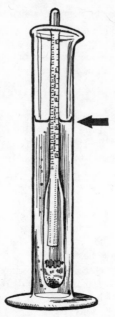

Fig. 13. The right way to read a hydrometer.

There are many ways the hydrometer can help you in your winemaking. Some specific uses follow.

Sugar Content of the Must

Some grapes, and all other fruits, have less than the optimum amount of sugar for winemaking. Grapes from very hot regions may have too much sugar. You need to know exactly how much sugar the must contains, so that you can raise or lower the proportion just enough to produce the type of wine you want.

The hydrometer will give you this information. The Balling scale produces a direct reading of percentage of sugar by weight; with a S.G. hydrometer, take a reading and consult the conversion table at the back of the book.

One correction is usually made in this determination (in

addition to the temperature correction, if that is needed). Grape juice and most other fermentable solutions contain not only sugar but also certain dissolved, non-fermentable solids such as colouring matter, acids, proteins, and so forth. So it is customary to subtract 1.6% from the apparent sugar content to get a correct figure for the percentage of sugar by weight. Laboratory analysis could give greater accuracy, but this method is good enough for even the most painstaking home winemaker.

To produce a dry red table wine your must should be about 23 to 24 Balling (S.G. 1.095 to 1.099). Dry white table wine needs a must of about 22 to 23 Balling (S.G. 1.090 to 1.095). For sweet wines you'll need a sweeter must, up to 28 Balling (S.G. 1.118). This will produce wine with 16% to 17% alcohol content by volume; it will require further sweetening to balance the high alcohol content and make a palatable beverage.

If your hydrometer indicates too little sugar in the must, correct by adding sugar. If you are aiming for more than 12% to 14% alcohol, the sugar should be added in two or three stages. Yeast cannot accept a high concentration of sugar present at any one time.

If a grape must has more sugar than you need, the remedy is to dilute the must with low-sugar grape juice if available, or with plain water. Add a little at a time, mix well, and test as you go.

Potential Alcohol Content

The potential alcohol content of a batch of must is the percentage of alcohol that will be produced if all the sugar is converted. In practice the potential is not always attained. The yeast may reach its limit of alcohol tolerance and stop fermenting while there is still unconsumed sugar.

But to find the alcohol potential, take a hydrometer reading of the unfermented must and consult the table at the back of the book.

Sugar Control During Fermentation

Your hydrometer will tell you how the fermentation is

progressing. Take readings daily during the primary fermentation. The S.G. should fall steadily, if all is going well. The recipes in Chapter 5 show you the initial and final readings to look for. If the S.G. refuses to drop to the desired level, the fermentation has "stuck," and you will have to take proper steps to get it going again (see Chapter 8). If the recipe calls for adding sugar in stages, the hydrometer will tell you when to do it, and will guide you in how much to add.

Determining the End of Fermentation

When the hydrometer reading falls to a fairly low figure and remains steady for a week or two, you can be reasonably sure that the fermentation is finished. This terminal hydrometer reading should always be less than 1.000 because of the low density of the alcohol. (The hydrometer alone will not disclose the proportion of sugar, if any, remaining in the wine at the close of fermentation. To find this figure you would need a sugar-analysis kit which uses a chemical reaction and a colour-matching chart to indicate unfermented sugar from 0.25% to 2%.)

Sugar Control For Sparkling Wines

The hydrometer is the most important piece of equipment for making sparkling or Champagne-type wines. You must have wine of a known alcoholic content (not over 11.5%) to begin with, and you depend on the hydrometer for this information. Full details of this procedure are given in Chapter 9.

ACID CONTROL

All fruits contain more or less acid. The sharp, sour taste of an unripe cherry or a stick of rhubarb comes from its containing much acid and little sugar. The mellow taste of a ripe apple comes from a higher proportion of sugar to acid. Yet it would not do to eliminate acid altogether. Too little acid produces a flat, insipid flavour or, at times, a bitter, medicinal-tasting wine. The right amount of acid helps to give a pleasing bite and tang to the flavour of a wine.

Many grapes, particularly those grown in the hotter areas

of California, are deficient in acid. Figs, dates and raisins contain practically none.

Acid-deficient fruit has three disadvantages for wine-making:

1. The must is more susceptible to contamination than one containing a proper amount of acid; vinegar and other spoilage bacteria thrive in a low-acid environment.

2. A low-acid wine is specially susceptible to oxidation, therefore has poor keeping qualities.

3. A low-acid wine will have a poor flavour.

On the other hand, northern-grown grapes, and such fruits as currants, cherries, gooseberries and elderberries, may contain excess acid. This tends to retard fermentation and may greatly increase the period before the wine becomes drinkable.

The Meaning of "Acid"

Grape-juice contains several organic acids. Malic, tartaric, citric, tannic and phosphoric are the most important. They are called the "fixed acids." Finished wine also contains "volatile acids" formed during fermentation, notably pro-prionic and acetic acids.

To measure these acids separately would take skill, equipment and time. Fortunately, that's not necessary. All we need for our purpose is to measure the total acids.

To draw a comparison, suppose your living-room, on a winter's evening, has hot-air registers going, an open fire burning, several electric lights and a TV set all giving off heat, and four people exhaling hot air. There's no need to measure the heat produced by each source separately: your thermostat measures the total heating effect from all sources and adjusts the furnace accordingly.

So we measure the total acids of a must or a finished wine and, for convenience, express the total *as if it were all one acid* instead of several.

Here we find a little international confusion. The French express total acids in terms of sulphuric acid, the British in terms of citric, and American and Canadian winemakers measure total acids as tartaric.

So remember that when we say a wine has .7% (or 7 parts per thousand) "acid as tartaric," we don't mean that it contains .7% tartaric acid and no other acids; we mean that the combined effect of all its acid ingredients is equivalent to that of .7% tartaric.

How Not to Measure Acids

You can't measure acids by tasting the must. With ripe fruits the acid content is masked, so far as human taste buds are concerned, by the large quantity of sugar that is present.

There's a chemical acidity measurement which is also unsuitable: the pH scale.

Keen gardeners will be familiar with pH as a measure of soil acidity or alkalinity. Efforts have been made to adapt the pH system for amateur winemakers. Slips of chemically treated paper, dipped in the must or wine, are supposed to show, by their colour changes, the pH of the solution.

The method would work well enough with simple solutions of acid and water. Unfortunately, fruit-juices and wines are not simple solutions. They contain substances—including pectin, sugar and tannin—which have a buffering effect that may result in pH being inadequate or misleading for the winemaker.

A Practical Test for Total Acids

A simple and accurate measurement of total acids can be made by the process of titration. That is, you take a measured quantity of must or wine and slowly add to it an alkaline solution of known strength. An indicating liquid called phenolphthalein shows, by turning from clear to pink, when all the acid has been neutralized. Then, by observing the amount of alkali used, you can tell how much acid was originally present. (The alkali reacts simultaneously with all the acids, giving the total-acids reading that you want.)

This titration process used to require fairly expensive laboratory equipment, but a cheap acid-testing kit is now on the market. It contains:

A 20 cc. graduated plastic syringe. This allows the precise

measuring of small quantities of liquid, which is the chief physical requirement for the test.

A small testing bottle.

A bottle of alkaline solution (sodium hydroxide, otherwise known as caustic soda).

A bottle of phenolphthalein colour indicator.

An eye-dropper.

Here is the procedure, beginning, of course, with syringe and testing bottle clean and dry. Let's assume, for the first example, that you are testing a white must or wine.

1. With the syringe measure 15 cc. of wine into the testing bottle.

2. With the eye-dropper add three drops of phenolphthalein solution to the bottle. Shake gently to mix the liquids. The phenolphthalein at this stage is clear, and remains clear as it mixes with the wine.

3. Wash out the syringe with water. Draw into it 10 cc. of the hydroxide solution.

4. Gently press the plunger and add 1 cc. of hydroxide to the testing bottle. You will see a pink streak at the point where the hydroxide enters the wine. Gently shake the bottle and the pink colour will clear away.

5. Add one more cc. of hydroxide and shake to clear the colour.

6. Continue adding hydroxide 1 cc. at a time until, on shaking, the colour does not clear, but the whole sample of wine becomes a uniform pink. (If the initial 10cc. of hydroxide fails to produce this change, take another 10 cc. into the syringe and continue.)

7. Note the number of cc. hydroxide used. Each cc. indicates .1% (one part per thousand) of acid as tartaric in the wine. That is if it takes 8 cc. of hydroxide to produce the colour change, the wine contains .8% acid as tartaric.

8. After the test, throw away the sample of wine and wash syringe, testing bottle and eye-dropper. Keep the hydroxide and phenolphthalein bottles well stoppered, since both solutions will deteriorate by exposure to air.

With red musts and wines the testing technique is identical, but the colour change is different. As each cc. of hydroxide is added you will see a purplish streak, noticeably darker than the red of the must. On shaking, this will at first disappear. The final colour change is to a dark grey that does not disappear on shaking.

In a thick red must, opaque with suspended matter, it may be hard to see the colour changes through the full diameter of the testing bottle. Then look at the top of the sample. As you shake the bottle, a little wave of liquid rises half an inch or so up the side of the bottle. Light shines easily through this wave, and reveals the colour changes clearly.

This method is cheap and easy. The quantity of chemicals supplied with the kit will do many tests, and you can buy refills cheaply. (To give accurate results the alkali must be the proper strength.)

The method is accurate enough as described but, if you wish, you can refine it a little. Fill the syringe with water and practice a slow, steady depression of the plunger until you can expel half a cc. at a time (Fig. 14). You can then get readings of acid to the second decimal place, *e.g.* .75%.

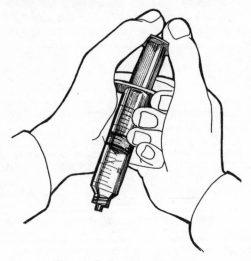

Fig. 14. Syringe for testing acid.

Significance of Acid Readings

The end purpose of acid control is to ensure good flavour and keeping qualities for your finished wines. So let's take a look at the acid content of various kinds of wines.

Popular California red table wines average .65% acid, California white table wines .7%, some of the famous German white wines as much as .95% acid.

Now we can begin to see how much acid we want in the must. First, let's consider that some acid is lost during the winemaking process, by precipitation of cream of tartar, and by conversion of some of the strong malic acid into the softer lactic acid. So you will need rather more acid in the must than you want to have in the finished wine.

For red grape table wine, start with .70% acid in the must. For white grape table wine start with .75% acid in the must. For fruit wines start with .60% acid. Fruit wines mature rapidly, so lose less acid in aging than do grape wines.

Acid in Winemaking Ingredients

California *vinifera* grapes rarely contain over .65% acid. Indeed, most *viniferas* available to amateurs have about .55% and some as little as .45%. Eastern and northern-grown hybrids will have more acid, often well over 1%. Other fruits are usually high in acid.

Test Before Fermentation

The time to measure and adjust the acid content of a must is before you add the yeast starter. Once the must begins fermenting, the carbon dioxide entrapped in it will produce false readings in the acid test.

To be sure, you can adjust acid after the wine is finished by blending with another finished wine, but by then you have lost all the benefits of having a correct acid balance throughout the fermentation period.

Correcting Acid Deficiencies

Suppose you test the fresh must and discover that it's short of acid. This is easily remedied by adding acid. You can get "acid blend" crystals at a winemakers' supply store. If the blend isn't available, tartaric acid alone will do.

Here are some figures that will show you how much acid to add.

Small quantities: 1/3 ounce acid added to 1 gallon of must raises the acid content by .3%.

Medium quantities: 1 ounce acid added to 6 gallons of must raises the acid content by .15%

Large quantities: 4 ounces acid added to 36 gallons of must raises the acid content by .1%.

Whatever quantity of must you are using, or whatever acid deficiency you find, you can work out the correct amount of acid to add by suitably adapting these figures. There's no need for elaborate juggling to get acid levels exactly to the recommended figures. Half a percentage point one way or the other won't spoil the wine, but as a general principle it's wise to be a little on the high side of the target rather than on the low side.

A useful precaution if you have a large volume of must is to stir it thoroughly to equalize the acidity and do the test three times, to be sure you get accurate results. It's easy enough to add acid, but taking it out is difficult.

Correcting Excess Acid

There are several methods of reducing excess acid, in the following order of preference:

1. The best method for use with grapes is to blend the high-acid grapes with others known to be low in acid. For example, a high-acid northern hybrid could be blended with a low-acid California *vinifera* (but foxy hybrids should not be blended with *viniferas*). This method is not always practicable because the amateur can't depend on getting exactly the kind of grapes he would like on the exact day when he needs them.

2. A very good substitute for grape-blending is to replace the low-acid fresh grape with reconstituted grape concentrate. These concentrates are usually as low as .35% acid. Simply reconstitute the concentrate with water according to the directions on the can and blend with the high-acid must.

Don't try blending the whole quantity of must at once. Take a measured sample—say a pint—and put it in a bottle. Add a measured quantity of the diluted concentrate, shake up the mixture, draw off 15 cc. and test for acidity. A few such trials will bring your sample to the right acidity, and simple arithmetic will tell you the quantities required for blending the whole batch.

3. This method is applicable only if you have cold weather in winter. Adjust the sugar to the desired level, but leave the acid alone; simply ferment the must with its high acid content. Then stand the wine outside or in an unheated shed for one to three weeks at temperatures between 25° and 35°F. The sharp cooling precipitates much of the acid as cream of tartar, hastens the aging process, and makes the wine drinkable sooner. But do not depend on chilling to remove excess acid over 1.0%. A must with more than that amount of acid should be ameliorated before fermentation.

4. Add water to the must until you have sufficiently reduced the acidity. Add sugar to raise the specific gravity back to the level you want. Then ferment. This method is used by some commercial wineries in the East. Obviously, it produces a thin wine, therefore it is better suited to white wines than to red.

5. Ferment the high-acid must as in Method 3, and then blend the finished wine with another wine that is low in acid. Here again, blend a small sample first, testing acidity and flavour as you go, to find the correct proportions.

6. Some winemakers neutralize excess acid with precipitated chalk, that is, pure calcium carbonate. But this method tends to leave an after-taste. Potassium bicarbonate is a better chemical to use, if you need to, but the method is seldom satisfactory and should be regarded as a last resort. Proper testing of the must before fermentation will avoid the need for it.

Suit Your Own Taste

The suggested acid levels for musts and wines will please the average palate, but you may find you like wines more or less acid than do most people.

If you buy a commercial wine that particularly pleases you, spare 15 cc. of it for a test of total acids, then guide your own production accordingly.

Keep records of all your winemaking operations and judge by taste the results of different degrees of acidity in the musts.

CONCLUSION

Reliable, trouble-free winemaking depends largely upon sugar and acid control. Carry out these simple procedures carefully. They will pay you rich dividends in economy of ingredients, and in the personal satisfaction that comes of making wine *as you like it, every time*.

5. Let's Make Wine

We've covered a lot of theory, so now let's get down to some practical work. Beginners should follow faithfully the recipes in this chapter. More experienced winemakers may try varying them to get wines exactly in accordance with their own tastes. In the last section of the chapter are some hints on writing your own recipes.

In some recipes, excessive lees or other factors cause a loss in racking, so that the yield in bottles does not equal the yield in gallons. Sparkling or Champagne wines are particularly susceptible to loss, in the process of being converted to Champagne.

All teaspoon measures in the recipes are level.

FRUIT WINES

Each recipe in this section makes 1 U.S. gallon of finished wine. There will be a little over a gallon at the start. Keep the extra wine apart, for topping up the secondary fermentor after racking.

The recipes can be multiplied as many times as you like.

For all fruit wines, use only sound, ripe fruit; reject unripe, mouldy or decaying fruit.

BANANA WINE

RECIPE 1

8 oz. dried bananas
1 lb. raisins
1 gal. warm water
2 lbs. white granulated sugar
1 Campden tablet
½ level tsp. yeast nutrient
3 level tsps. acid blend
Wine yeast

RECIPE 2

8 oz. dried bananas
1 6-oz. can frozen orange juice
1 gal. warm water
2½ lbs. white granulated sugar
1 Campden tablet
1 level tsp. acid blend
¼ tsp. grape tannin
½ level tsp. yeast nutrient
Wine yeast

Chop raisins and bananas. Mix all ingredients except wine yeast in primary fermentor. When must is cool (70-75°F.) add yeast. Cover with plastic sheet. Stir daily. Ferment for 6-7 days in primary fermentor then strain out solids and siphon into gallon jugs or carboy. Attach fermentation locks. Rack in 3 weeks and again in 3 months. When wine is clear and stable, add 1 Campden tablet and 1 Wine-Art Antioxidant tablet per gallon and bottle.

Age 10 months.

ELDERBERRY WINE

RECIPE 3	RECIPE 3a
6 oz. dried elderberries	6 oz. dried elderberries
1 lb. raisins	8 oz. dried bananas
1 gal. water	1 gal. water
2 lbs. white granulated sugar	3 lbs. white granulated sugar
½ level tsp. yeast nutrient	½ level tsp. yeast nutrient
3 level tsps. acid blend	3 level tsps. acid blend
1 Campden tablet	1 Campden tablet
Wine yeast	Wine yeast

Chop raisins and bananas. Mix all ingredients except wine yeast in primary fermentor. When must is cool (70-75°F.) add yeast. Cover with plastic sheet. Stir daily. Ferment for 6-7 days in primary fermentor then strain out solids and siphon into gallon jugs or carboy. Attach fermentation locks. Rack in 3 weeks and again in 3 months. When wine is clear and stable, add 1 Campden tablet and 1 Wine-Art Antioxidant tablet per gallon and bottle.

Age 10 months.

BLACKBERRY OR LOGANBERRY WINE

RECIPES 4 & 4a

4 lbs. blackberries *or*
2 lbs. loganberries
2½ lbs. white granulated sugar
1 gal. water
1 level tsp. yeast nutrient

1 level tsp. acid blend
1 Campden tablet
½ tsp. pectic enzyme powder
Wine yeast

Starting specific gravity should be 1.090 - 1.095, acid .65%.

Use only sound ripe berries. Crush fruit and put all ingredients except wine yeast in primary fermentor. Add hot water and stir to dissolve sugar. Cover with plastic sheet. When must is cool (70-75°F.) add yeast. Stir the must daily. Ferment 5-6 days or until specific gravity is 1.040. Strain out fruit pulp and press. Siphon into gallon jugs or carboys and attach fermentation locks. Rack in three weeks and again in three months. When wine is clear and stable, bottle. Wine may be sweetened to taste at time of bottling with sugar syrup (2 parts sugar to 1 part water). Add 2 Wine-Art Stabilizer tablets to prevent renewed fermentation.

Age 1 year.

RASPBERRY OR STRAWBERRY WINE

RECIPES 5 & 5a

2½ lbs. raspberries *or*	½ level tsp. acid blend
3½ lbs. strawberries	1 Campden tablet
2 lbs. white granulated sugar	½ tsp. pectic enzyme powder
1 gal. water	Wine yeast
1 level tsp. yeast nutrient	

Starting specific gravity should be 1.090 - 1.095, acid .65%.

Use only sound ripe berries. Crush fruit and put all ingredients except wine yeast in primary fermentor. Add hot water and stir to dissolve sugar. Cover with plastic sheet. When must is cool (70-75°F.) add yeast. Stir the must daily. Ferment 5-6 days or until specific gravity is 1.040. Strain out fruit pulp and press. Siphon into gallon jugs or carboys and attach fermentation locks. Rack in 3 weeks and again in 3 months. When wine is clear and stable, bottle. Wine may be sweetened to taste at time of bottling with sugar syrup (2 parts sugar to 1 part water). Add 2 Wine-Art Stabilizer tablets to prevent renewed fermentation.

Age 1 year.

BLUEBERRY WINE

RECIPE 6

2 lbs. Blueberries
1 lb. Raisins
2 lbs. white granulated sugar
1 gal. water
1½ level tsps. acid blend

½ tsp. yeast energizer
½ tsp. pectic enzyme powder
1 Campden tablet
Wine yeast

Starting specific gravity should be 1.090 - 1.095, acid .65%.

Use only sound ripe fruit. Crush fruit and put all ingredients except wine yeast in primary fermentor. Add hot water and stir to dissolve sugar. Cover with plastic sheet. When must is cool (70-75°F.) add yeast. Stir the must daily. Ferment for 5-6 days or until specific gravity is 1.040. Strain out fruit pulp and press. Siphon into gallon jugs or carboy and attach fermentation locks. Rack in 3 weeks and again in 3 months. When wine is clear and stable, bottle. Wine may be sweetened to taste at time of bottling with sugar syrup (2 parts sugar to 1 part water). Add 2 Wine-Art Stabilizer tablets to prevent renewed fermentation.

Age 1 year.

CHERRY WINE

RECIPE 7

3 lbs. sweet cherries *or*
2 lbs. sour cherries
2½ lbs. white granulated sugar
2 level tsps. acid blend
1 Campden tablet

1 level tsp. yeast nutrient
½ tsp. pectic enzyme powder
1 gal. water
Wine yeast

Starting specific gravity should be 1.090 - 1.095, acid .65%.

Use only sound ripe fruit and remove stems and leaves. Crush cherries and put all ingredients except wine yeast in primary fermentor. Add hot water and stir to dissolve sugar. Cover with plastic sheet. When must is cool (70-75°F.) add yeast. Stir the must daily. Ferment for 5-6 days or until specific gravity is 1.040. Strain out fruit pulp and press. Siphon into gallon jugs or carboys and attach fermentation locks. Rack in 3 weeks and again in 3 months. When wine is clear and stable, bottle. Wine may be sweetened to taste at time of bottling with sugar syrup (2 parts sugar to 1 part water). Add 2 Wine-Art Stabilizer tablets per gallon to prevent renewed fermentation.

Age 1 year.

CHOKE CHERRY WINE

RECIPE 8

2 lbs. choke cherries	1 level tsp. yeast nutrient
1 lb. raisins (chopped)	½ tsp. pectic enzyme powder
2½ lbs. white granulated sugar	1 level tsp. acid blend
1 gal. water	Wine yeast
1 Campden tablet	

Starting specific gravity should be 1.100 to 1.105, acid .65%.

Use only sound ripe fruit and remove stems and leaves. Crush cherries but do not break pits. Put crushed fruit and sugar in primary fermentor. Cover with plastic sheet and leave overnight. Next day add all other ingredients except yeast. Stir to dissolve sugar. When must is cool (70-75°F.) add yeast. Stir the must daily. Ferment for 5-6 days or until specific gravity is 1.040. Strain out fruit pulp and siphon into gallon jugs or carboys. Attach fermentation locks. Rack in 3 weeks and again in 3 months. When wine is clear and stable, bottle. Wine may be sweetened to taste at time of bottling with sugar syrup (2 parts sugar to 1 part water). Add 2 Wine-Art Stabilizer tablets to prevent renewed fermentation.

Age 1 year.

DANDELION WINE

RECIPE 9

6 cups dandelion petals
2 lbs. white granulated sugar
1 lb. light raisins
3 level tsps. acid blend
1 Campden tablet

½ tsp. yeast energizer
1 gal. hot water
¼ tsp. grape tannin
Wine yeast

Use only dandelion petals. Cut up raisins and put all ingredients except wine yeast in primary fermentor. Pour gallon of *hot* water over ingredients and stir to dissolve sugar. Cover with plastic sheet. Add yeast when must is cool (70-75°F.) Ferment for 3 days, strain, siphon into gallon jugs or carboy and attach fermentation lock. Rack in 3 weeks. Make sure all containers are topped up. Rack again in 3 months. When wine is clear and stable, bottle. To prevent oxidation add 1 antioxidant tablet per gallon, or 1 level teaspoon ascorbic acid per 6 gallons.

Age 6 months.

2nd Run
2 gal.
8/23/79 - 1.090
9/5/79 - Racked - 1.040
10/9/79 Racked
1/19/80 Bottled

PEACH OR APRICOT WINE

❦

RECIPES 10 & 10a

2½ lbs. peaches *or* apricots
2 lbs. white granulated sugar
1 gal. water
1 level tsp. yeast nutrient
1½ level tsps. acid blend

1 Campden tablet
½ tsp. pectic enzyme powder
¼ tsp. grape tannin
Wine yeast

Starting Specific Gravity should be 1.090 - 1.095, acid .65%.

Use only sound ripe fruit and remove the stones. Crush
fruit and put all ingredients except yeast in primary fermentor. Add hot water and stir to dissolve sugar. Cover with
plastic sheet. When must is cool (70-75°F.) add yeast. Stir
the must daily. Ferment for 5-6 days or until specific gravity
is 1.040. Strain out fruit pulp and press. Siphon into gallon
jugs or carboys and attach fermentation locks. Rack in 3
weeks and again in 3 months. Fine with Serena Finings and
when wine is clear and stable, bottle. To preserve flavour and
colour add 1 Wine-Art Antioxidant tablet per gallon at time
of bottling. Wine may be sweetened to taste at time of bottling
with sugar syrup (2 parts sugar to 1 part water). Add 2
Wine-Art Stabilizer tablets to prevent renewed fermentation.

Age 1 year.

Apricot

7/22/79 - 1.090
7/25/79 - Racked - 1.040
8/12/79 Racked - .990
9/18/79 Racked
Bottled 12/23/79
2 cups sugar water.

Peach

8/19/79 - 1.090
8/21/79 1.068
8/23/79 Racked - 1.0
10/9/79 - Racked
1/19/80 - Bottled

12 Bottles

5 lbs

2 1/4
8
8 9 *2 1/8*

PLUM WINE

❧

RECIPE 11

2½ lbs. plums	½ tsp. pectic enzyme powder
2½ lbs. white granulated sugar	1 Campden tablet
1 gal. of water	1½ level tsps. acid blend
½ level tsp. yeast nutrient	Wine yeast

Starting Specific Gravity should be 1.090 - 1.095, acid .65%.

Use only sound ripe fruit. Remove stones and crush plums. Put all ingredients except wine yeast in primary fermentor. Add hot water and stir to dissolve sugar. Cover with plastic sheet. When must is cool (70-75°F.) add yeast. Stir the must daily. Ferment 5-6 days or until specific gravity is 1.040. Strain out fruit pulp and press. Siphon into gallon jugs or carboys and attach fermentation locks. Rack in 3 weeks and again in 3 months. When wine is clear and stable, bottle. Wine may be sweetened to taste at time of bottling with sugar syrup (2 parts sugar to 1 part water). Add 2 Wine-Art Stabilizer tablets to prevent renewed fermentation.

Age 1 year.

7/16/79 - started - 1.095
7/21/79 1.050
7/22/79 - 1.040 - Racked -
8/12/79 Racked - .990
Bottled - 11/21/79
3/4 c. Sugo-water per 2 gal.
c Sugwate 1 3/4 gal.
14 Bottles

RAISIN WINE

RECIPE 12

2 lbs. raisins
1 gal. warm water
2 lbs. white granulated sugar
½ level tsp. yeast nutrient

4 level tsps. acid blend
1 Campden tablet
Wine yeast

Chop raisins. Mix all ingredients except wine yeast in primary fermentor. When must is cool (70-75°F.) add yeast. Cover with plastic sheet. Stir daily for 5 or 6 days. Remove raisins and press. Siphon into gallon jug or carboy and attach fermentation lock. Rack in 3 weeks. Make sure container is topped up. Rack again in 3 months. When wine is clear and stable, bottle.

Age 6 months.

RHUBARB WINE

RECIPE 13

2½ lbs. rhubarb
2½ lbs. white granulated sugar
1 level tsp. yeast nutrient
1 gal. water

1 Campden tablet
¼ tsp. grape tannin
Wine yeast

Cut up rhubarb and put in primary fermentor. Pour dry sugar over fruit to extract juice. Cover with plastic sheet and allow to stand 24 hours. Add all other ingredients including wine yeast. Ferment 48 hours. Strain out pulp and press as dry as possible. In 3 or 4 days syphon into gallon jugs or carboy and attach fermentation lock. Rack in 3 weeks. Make sure all containers are topped up. Rack again in 3 months. When wine is clear and stable, bottle. Wine may be sweetened to taste at time of bottling with sugar syrup (2 parts sugar to 1 part water). Add 2 Wine-Art Stabilizer tablets per gallon to prevent renewed fermentation. To preserve colour and flavour add 1 Wine-Art Antioxidant tablet per gallon.

Age 6 months.

WINE-ART DRIED ROSE HIP WINE

RECIPE 14

6 oz. dried rose hips
8 oz. raisins
1 Campden tablet
1 gal. *hot* water

½ oz. acid blend
½ tsp. yeast nutrient
2 lbs. white granulated sugar
Wine yeast

Mix all ingredients except yeast in primary fermentor. Cover with plastic sheet. When must is cool (70-75°F.) add yeast. Stir daily. Ferment for 5-6 days, strain out rose hips, siphon into gallon jug and attach fermentation lock. Rack in 3 weeks and again in 3 months. When wine is clear and stable add 1 Campden tablet and 1 Wine-Art antioxidant tablet per gallon and bottle.

Age 6 months.

GOOSEBERRY WINE

✳

RECIPE 15

2½ lbs. Gooseberries
2 lbs. white granulated sugar
1 gal. water
1 Campden tablet
½ level tsp. acid blend

½ level tsp. yeast nutrient
¼ tsp. grape tannin
½ tsp. pectic enzyme powder
Wine yeast

Starting Specific Gravity should be 1.080 - 1.085, acid .7%.

Crush gooseberries, add sugar, Campden tablets and pectic enzyme powder. Mix thoroughly in primary fermentor. Cover with plastic sheet and allow to stand for 12 hours to extract juice. Add warm water and all other ingredients except yeast. When temperature is cool (70-75°F.) add yeast. Ferment for 2 days then strain out pulp and press as dry as possible. Ferment for 2 more days then siphon into gallon jugs or carboy and attach fermentation lock. Rack in 3 weeks and again in 3 months. When wine is clear and stable, bottle.

Sparkling Wine

This recipe will give you dry white table wine which can be made into a sparkling wine by following the directions for Champagne (Chapter 9).

Sauterne-style Wine

Add one additional pound of sugar to basic recipe. When wine is ready to bottle, sweeten to taste with sugar syrup (2 parts sugar to 1 part water). Add 2 Wine-Art Stabilizer tablets per gallon to prevent renewed fermentation.

Age 1 year.

ORANGE WINE

※

RECIPE 16

2 6-oz. cans frozen orange juice
1 gal warm water
1 orange, sliced
1 lb. chopped raisins

1 Campden tablet
2 lbs. white sugar
½ level tsp. yeast nutrient
Wine yeast

Mix all ingredients except wine yeast in primary fermentor. Cover with plastic sheet. Add yeast when must is cool (70-75°F.) Stir once daily for 7 days. Siphon into gallon jug and attach fermentation lock. Rack in 3 weeks. Add 1 Campden tablet and top up jug (use water if necessary). Rack again in 3 months. When wine is clear and stable, bottle.

Age 1 year.

APPLE OR PEAR WINE

✻

RECIPES 17 & 17a

6 lbs. apples *or*
4 lbs. pears
2 lbs. white granulated sugar
1 Campden tablet
1 level tsp. yeast nutrient
½ oz. acid blend

1 gal. water
½ tsp. pectic enzyme powder
¼ tsp. grape tannin
   (omit in Pear Wine)
Wine yeast

Starting Specific Gravity should be 1.090 - 1.100, acid .65%.

If possible the apples or pears should be crushed, pressed and just the juice used, otherwise chop fruit and put all ingredients except yeast in primary fermentor. Mix well. When must is cool (70-75°F.) add yeast. Cover with plastic sheet and ferment for 4-5 days or until specific gravity is 1.040. Strain out fruit and press. Siphon into gallon jugs or carboy and attach fermentation locks. Rack in 3 weeks and again in 3 months. Fine with Sparkolloid and when wine is clear and stable, bottle. Add 1 Wine-Art Antioxidant tablet per gallon when bottling to preserve colour and flavour. Wine may be sweetened to taste at time of bottling with sugar syrup (2 parts sugar to 1 part water). Add 2 Wine-Art Stabilizer tablets to prevent renewed fermentation.

Age 1 year.

CRAB APPLE WINE

RECIPE 18

4 lbs. crab apples
1 gal. water
1 lb. raisins
2 lbs. white granulated sugar
½ level tsp. acid blend

½ level tsp. yeast nutrient
½ tsp. pectic enzyme powder
1 Campden tablet
Wine yeast

Starting Specific Gravity should be 1.095 - 1.100, acid .65%.

Chop apples and raisins. Put all ingredients except yeast in primary fermentor. Stir to dissolve sugar. Cover with plastic sheet. When must is cool (70-75°F.) add yeast. Stir the must daily. Ferment for 5-6 days or until specific gravity is 1.040. Strain out fruit pulp and press. Siphon into gallon jugs or carboy and attach fermentation locks. Rack in 3 weeks and again in 3 months. When wine is clear and stable, add 1 Wine-Art Antioxidant tablet per gallon and bottle.

Age 1 year.

APPLE CIDER

RECIPE 19

1 gal. fresh apple juice*	¼ tsp. grape tannin
Sugar to S.G. 1.060	¼ tsp. yeast energizer
½ tsp. pectic enzyme powder	1 Campden tablet
½ level tsp. acid blend	Wine yeast

*Depending upon the variety of apple, you will require 14 to 16 pounds of fruit for 1 gallon of juice. A blend of bitter and sweet apples will give best results.

Starting specific gravity should be 1.060, acid .5%.

Crush apples. Dissolve Campden tablets in small amount of water and stir into crushed apples. Put crushed apples into a nylon or cheesecloth bag and press as dry as possible. Allow juice to settle overnight in primary fermentor covered with a plastic sheet. Next day siphon carefully to remove juice from apple solids. Adjust the sugar so that the starting specific gravity is 1.060. Add all the other ingredients including the yeast. Ferment in primary fermentor for 3-5 days or until specific gravity is 1.020. Siphon into gallon jugs or carboy and attach fermentation locks. Rack in approximately 3 weeks, when specific gravity is 1.000, and add 1 Wine-Art Antioxidant tablet per gallon. When cider is clear and stable, siphon into primary fermentor. For each gallon of cider dissolve 2 oz. white sugar and stir in gently. Siphon cider into bottles and cap with crown caps.

Age 3 months.

CRANBERRY WINE

RECIPE 20

3 lbs. cranberries	1 Campden tablet
1 lb. raisins	1 level tsp. yeast nutrient
3 lbs. white granulated sugar	½ tsp. pectic enzyme powder
1 gal. water	Wine yeast

Starting Specific Gravity should be 1.110 - 1.115, acid .65%.

Crush cranberries and chop raisins. Put all ingredients except wine yeast in primary fermentor. Add warm water and stir to dissolve sugar. When must is cool (70-75°F.) add yeast. Cover with plastic sheet and stir daily. Ferment in primary fermentor for 5-6 days or until specific gravity is 1.040. Strain out cranberries and raisins and press as dry as possible. Siphon into gallon jugs or carboy and attach fermentation locks. Rack in 3 weeks. When wine is clear and stable, bottle. This will be a strong, medium-sweet wine.

Age 1 year.

BLACK CURRANT WINE

RECIPE 21

2 lbs. black currants
2½ lbs. white granulated sugar
1 gal. water
1 Campden tablet

1 level tsp. yeast nutrient
½ tsp. pectic enzyme powder
Wine yeast

Starting Specific Gravity should be 1.100 - 1.110, acid .65%.

Use only sound ripe fruit. Discard any leaves or stems. Crush black currants and put all ingredients except yeast in primary fermentor. Add hot water and stir to dissolve sugar. Cover with plastic sheet. When must is cool (70-75°F.) add yeast. Stir the must daily. Ferment for 5-6 days or until specific gravity is 1.040. Strain out fruit. Siphon into gallon jugs or carboy and attach fermentation lock. Rack in 3 weeks and again in 3 months. When wine is clear and stable, bottle. This is a slightly sweet, very fruity wine.

Age 10 months.

FRUIT CONCENTRATES

Many people make their first wines from fresh fruit, but the easiest way to start is with fruit concentrates. In Chapter 3 we have seen the many advantages these concentrates offer the winemaker. They are now available nearly everywhere. The following recipes will give you an idea of the variety of wines you can make from concentrates.

Most of the recipes use three-quart cans of concentrate. Naturally, you may multiply a recipe as many times as you wish, but be sure before buying and mixing the ingredients that your primary fermentor is big enough. For 5 gallons of must you need at least a 7-gallon fermentor, and so in proportion for larger volumes.

APRICOT WINE BASE

✻

RECIPE 22

1 3-qt. can Apricot Wine Base
7 cans warm water
17 lbs. granulated white sugar
2 level teaspoons pectic enzyme pdr.
1 oz. yeast nutrient

5 Campden tablets
2½ ounces acid blend
½ teaspoon grape tannin
Wine yeast

YIELD

6 gallons (30 25-oz. bottles) strong, semi-sweet, Sauterne-type wine.

Mix all ingredients except wine yeast in primary fermentor. When must is cool (70-75 degrees F.) add yeast. Cover with plastic sheet. Stir the must daily. Ferment in primary fermentor for 4 to 5 days or until specific gravity is 1.040. Strain out fruit pulp, syphon into gallon jugs and attach fermentation locks. Rack in three weeks and again in three months. When wine is clear and stable, bottle. If necessary sweeten to taste with sugar syrup (2 parts sugar to 1 part water). Add 2 Stabilizer tablets per gallon to prevent renewed fermentation.

Dry Wine

Reduce total amount of sugar from 17 pounds to 10 pounds.

Sparkling Wine

Reduce total amount of sugar to 10 pounds. In approximately 3 months when wine is clear and stable it may be made into a sparkling wine by following the directions for Champagne (Chapter 9).

Age 3 months.

WINE-ART BLACKBERRY WINE BASE

RECIPE 23

1 3-qt. can Blackberry Wine Base
4 cans water
9 level tsps. acid blend
3 Campden tablets
1 lb. raisins

10 lbs. white granulated sugar
1 level tsp. pectic enzyme powder
3 level tsps. yeast nutrient
1 pkt. Andovin Wine Yeast

YIELD
3½ gallons (18 25-oz. bottles) full-bodied, medium-sweet wine.

Mix all ingredients except yeast in primary fermentor. When must is cool (70-75°F.) add yeast. Cover with plastic sheet. Ferment in primary fermentor for 5-6 days. Strain out fruit and raisins. Siphon into gallon jugs and attach fermentation locks. Rack in 2 weeks and again in 2 months. When wine is clear and stable, bottle. If necessary sweeten to taste with sugar syrup (2 parts sugar to 1 part water). Add 2 Wine-Art Stabilizer tablets per gallon to prevent renewed fermentation.

Dry Wine

For a full-bodied dry wine reduce sugar to 7½ pounds.

Age 6 months.

WINE-ART CHERRY WINE BASE

※

RECIPE 24

1 3-qt. can Cherry Wine Base
5 cans warm water
7 lbs. granulated white sugar
4 levels tsps. yeast nutrient
2 oz. acid blend

½ tsp. grape tannin
2 level tsps. pectic enzyme powder
5 Campden tablets
Wine yeast

YIELD

4½ gallons (24 25-oz. bottles) dry, still or sparkling rosé wine.

Mix all ingredients except wine yeast in primary fermentor. When must is cool (70-75°F.) add yeast. Cover with plastic sheet. Ferment in primary fermentor for two days. Remove cherry pulp and press. Ferment for two more days. Siphon into gallon jugs and attach fermentation locks. Rack in 3 weeks. Rack again in 3 months. Wine may be sweetened to taste at time of bottling with sugar syrup (2 parts sugar to 1 part water). Add 2 Wine-Art Stabilizer tablets per gallon to prevent renewed fermentation.

Crackling Rosé

When fermentation has stopped add 3 oz. sugar syrup (2 parts sugar to 1 part water) to each gallon. Mix thoroughly. Bottle in tall (30-oz) pop bottles with crown caps or in champagne bottles with plastic stoppers and wires. This wine will have a slight but firm yeast deposit.

Age 6 months.

WINE-ART MONTMORENCY CHERRY WINE BASE

RECIPE 25

1 3-qt. can Montmorency Cherry Base	1½ tsps. pectic enzyme powder
4 cans water	½ tsp. grape tannin
10 lbs. white granulated sugar	1½ oz. acid blend
2 lbs. raisins	3 Campden tablets
1 tsp. yeast energizer	Wine yeast

YIELD

3½ gallons (18 25-oz. bottles) light, sweet, aromatic wine.

Chop raisins and mix all ingredients except yeast in primary fermentor. When must is cool (70-75°F.) add yeast. Cover with plastic sheet. Stir daily. Ferment in primary fermentor for 5-6 days or until specific gravity is 1.040. Strain out fruit, siphon into gallon jugs and attach fermentation locks. Rack in 3 weeks and again in 3 months. When wine is clear and stable, bottle. Wine may be sweetened to taste at time of bottling with sugar syrup (2 parts sugar to 1 part water). Add 2 Wine-Art Stabilizer tablets per gallon to prevent renewed fermentation.

Age 10 months.

WINE-ART PEACH WINE BASE

RECIPE 26

1 3-qt. can Peach Wine Base	2½ tsps. pectic enzyme powder
7 cans warm water	5 Campden tablets
12 lbs. white granulated sugar	½ tsp. grape tannin
2 oz. acid blend	Wine yeast
1 oz yeast nutrient	

YIELD
6 gallons (30 25-oz. bottles) dry white wine.

Mix all ingredients except wine yeast in primary fermentor. When must is cool (70-75°F.) add yeast. Cover with plastic sheet. Ferment in primary fermentor for 5 days. Remove peach pulp and press. Siphon into gallon jugs or carboy and attach fermentation locks. Rack in 3 months. When wine is clear and stable, bottle. To preserve flavour and colour add 1 Wine-Art Antioxidant tablet per gallon at time of bottling. Wine may be sweetened to taste at time of bottling with sugar syrup (2 parts sugar to 1 part water). Add 2 Wine-Art Stabilizer tablets per gallon to prevent renewed fermentation.

Age 9 months.

WINE-ART PLUM WINE BASE

RECIPE 27

1 3-qt. can Plum Wine Base
5½ cans water
5 Campden tablets
10 lbs. white granulated sugar
2 oz. acid blend

2½ tsps pectic enzyme powder
½ tsp. grape tannin
4 level tsps. yeast nutrient
1 pkt. Andovin Wine Yeast

YIELD

4½ gallons (24 25-oz. bottles).

Mix all ingredients except yeast in primary fermentor. When must is cool (70-75°F.) add yeast. Cover with plastic sheet. Ferment in primary fermentor for 5-6 days. Strain out fruit, siphon into gallon jugs or carboy and attach fermentation locks. Rack in 3 weeks and again in 3 months. Fine with Sparkolloid Tablets and sweeten to taste with sugar syrup (2 parts sugar to 1 part water). Add 2 Wine-Art Stabilizer tablets per gallon to prevent renewed fermentation.

Age 6 months.

WINE-ART GOTA DE ORO MEAD, OR HONEY WINE

RECIPE 28

1 28-ounce can Mead Base
3½ cans water
4 level tsps. acid blend
1 level tsp. yeast nutrient

¼ tsp. grape tannin
1 Campden tablet
Wine yeast

YIELD

1 gallon (5 25-oz. bottles) dry, white wine.

Mix all ingredients except yeast in primary fermentor. When must is cool (70-75°F.) add yeast. Ferment for 5 days, then siphon into gallon jug and attach fermentation lock. Rack when fermentation stops. Top up with water and add 1 crushed Wine-Art Antioxidant tablet per gallon and bottle.

Age 1 year.

SUMMER CIDER

RECIPE 29

1 3-qt. can Apple Concentrate	½ tsp. grape tannin
9 cans water	1 oz. acid blend
6 Campden tablets	2 level tsps. yeast energizer
3 level tsps. pectic enzyme powder	2 pkts. Andovin Wine Yeast

YIELD

7½ gallons (80 12-oz. bottles) light, dry, sparkling cider.
Age 3 months

CHRISTMAS CIDER

RECIPE 29a

1 3-qt. can Apple Concentrate	½ tsp. grape tannin
7 cans water	5 level tsps. acid blend
5 Campden tablets	2 level tsps. yeast energizer
2 level tsps. pectic enzyme powder	1 pkt. Andovin Wine Yeast

YIELD

6 gallons (60 12-oz. bottles) dry, sparkling cider.
Age 6 months

Mix all ingredients except yeast in primary fermentor. Cover with plastic sheet. When must is cool (70-75°F.) add yeast. Ferment for 5-6 days or until specific gravity is 1.015. Siphon into gallon jugs or carboy and attach fermentation locks. When specific gravity is .997-1.000 siphon back into primary fermentor. Add 1 Wine-Art Antioxidant tablet and 2 oz. cane sugar per gallon. Stir gently to mix. Siphon into beer bottles and cap with crown caps.

GRAPE CONCENTRATES

The best grape concentrates available come from Spain and California. With these concentrates you can produce a light or a full-bodied dry table wine, a Champagne-style wine or a Sparkling Burgundy, a sweet Port or a Sherry-style wine.

These concentrates are versatile and you can make a wine to suit every palate.

WINE-ART CALIFORNIA WHITE GRAPE CONCENTRATE

RECIPE 30

1 1-gal. can White Grape Concentrate	4 Campden tablets
4 cans water	½ tsp. grape tannin
2 lbs. white granulated sugar	4 level tsp. yeast nutrient
2 oz. acid blend	1 pkt. Andovin Wine Yeast

YIELD

5 gallons (24 25-oz. bottles) full-bodied, dry, white table wine.

RECIPE 30a

1 1-gal. can White Grape Concentrate	12 lbs. white granulated sugar
9 cans water	2 level tsps. grape tannin
8 Campden tablets	5 oz. acid blend
1 oz. yeast nutrient	2 pkts. Andovin Wine Yeast

YIELD

10 gallons (48 25-oz. bottles) light-bodied, dry table wine.

Mix all ingredients except yeast in primary fermentor. When must is cool (70-75°F.) add yeast. Cover with plastic sheet. Ferment in primary fermentor 6-7 days or until specific gravity is 1.030. Siphon into gallon jugs or carboys and attach fermentation locks. Rack in 3 weeks and again in 3 months. Fine with Serena Finings and bottle. Wine may be sweetened to taste at time of bottling with sugar syrup (2 parts sugar to 1 part water). Add 2 Wine-Art Stabilizer tablets per gallon to prevent renewed fermentation.

Age 6 months.

WINE-ART CALIFORNIA RED GRAPE CONCENTRATE

RECIPE 31

1 1-gal. can Red Grape
Concentrate
4 cans water
2 lbs. white granulated sugar
2 oz. acid blend

4 Campden tablets
½ tsp. grape tannin
4 level tsp. yeast nutrient
1 pkt. Andovin Wine Yeast

YIELD
5 gallons (24 25-oz. bottles) full-bodied, dry, red table wine.

RECIPE 31a

1 1-gal. can Red Grape
Concentrate
9 cans water
8 Campden tablets
1 oz. yeast nutrient

12 lbs. white granulated sugar
2 level tsps. grape tannin
5 oz. acid blend
2 pkts. Andovin Wine Yeast

YIELD
10 gallons (48 25-oz. bottles) light-bodied, dry, red table wine.

Mix all ingredients except yeast in primary fermentor. When must is cool (70-75°F.) add yeast. Cover with plastic sheet. Ferment in primary fermentor 6-7 days or until specific gravity is 1.030. Siphon into gallon jugs or carboys and attach fermentation locks. Rack in 3 weeks and again in 3 months. Fine with Serena Finings and bottle. Wine may be sweetened to taste at time of bottling with sugar syrup (2 parts sugar to 1 part water). Add 2 Wine-Art stabilizer tablets per gallon to prevent renewed fermentation.

Age 6 months.

SHERRY

RECIPE 32

1 76-oz. can Spanish Fig
Concentrate
1 1-gal. can California White
Grape Concentrate
9 gals. warm water
15 lbs. white granulated sugar

5 oz. acid blend
2 level tsps. yeast energizer
2 level tsps. grape tannin
4 8-oz. packages dried bananas
10 Campden tablets
Sherry Yeast (40-oz. starter)

10 additional lbs. white sugar, to be added in two stages

YIELD
13 gallons (60 25-oz. bottles) full-bodied, sweet, Sherry-type wine.

Prepare Sherry Yeast starter according to instructions, 3 days in advance.

Separate bananas and mix all ingredients except wine yeast in primary fermentor. When must is cool (70-75°F.) add yeast. Cover with plastic sheet. Stir gently once a day. Ferment 5-7 days or until specific gravity is 1.040. Withdraw 6 cups of wine and dissolve additional 5 lbs. of sugar. Stir into primary fermentor and allow to ferment 2-3 days or until specific gravity is 1.030. Remove bananas, siphon into gallon jugs or carboys and attach fermentation locks. When specific gravity is 1.010 another 5 lbs. of sugar can be dissolved and added. Finished wine will have alcohol content of 17% to 18% by volume. Rack when fermentation has stopped and wine is clear. Specific gravity should be 1.000.

More Sherry flavour can be produced by keeping the wine at a temperature of 110-130°F. for 2-3 months. Place your gallon jugs or carboys in a cardboard carton with a 60- or 100-watt light bulb. Care must be taken to guard against fire hazards. Fine finished wine. Sweeten to taste with sugar syrup (2 parts sugar to 1 part water). Fortify with 2 oz. Brandy per 25-oz. bottle.

Age 1 year. Will keep 5 to 10 years.

PORT WINE

RECIPE 33

1 1-gal. can California Red Grape Concentrate
5 cans warm water
6 lbs. white granulated sugar
6 oz. dried elderberries
2 8-oz. packages dried bananas
6 lbs. white sugar to be added in two stages

2 level tsps. yeast energizer
3 oz. acid blend
5 Campden tablets
Port yeast

YIELD
6 gallons (30 25-oz. bottles) full-bodied, sweet, Port-style wine.

Prepare Port Yeast starter according to instructions, 3 days in advance.

Separate bananas and mix all ingredients except wine yeast in primary fermentor. When must is cool (70-75°F.) add yeast. Cover with plastic sheet. Stir gently once a day. When specific gravity is 1.040 withdraw four cups of must and dissolve additional three lbs. of sugar. Stir into primary fermentor. When specific gravity is 1.030 strain out elderberries and bananas and siphon into gallon jugs or carboy. Attach fermentation locks. Wine should not be left in primary fermentor for more than 7 days.

When specific gravity is 1.010 another three pounds of sugar can be dissolved and added. Rack when fermentation has stopped. Fine finished wine with Sparkolloid tablets. Sweeten to taste with sugar syrup (2 parts sugar to 1 part water.) Fortify with 2 oz. Brandy per 25-ounce bottle.

Age 1 year.

SPARKLING BURGUNDY

RECIPE 34

1 1-gal. can California Red Grape Concentrate
5 cans water
3 oz. acid blend
3 lbs. white granulated sugar

1 level tsp. yeast energizer
5 Campden tablets
1 pkt. Andovin Wine Yeast

Starting specific gravity should be 1.080, acid .70%.

YIELD
6 gallons (30 25-oz. bottles) sparkling red wine.

Mix all ingredients except wine yeast in primary fermentor. When must is cool (70-75°F.) add yeast. Cover with plastic sheet. Ferment in primary fermentor 6-7 days or until specific gravity is 1.030. Siphon into gallon jugs or carboys and attach fermentation lock. Rack in 3 weeks. Rack again in 3 months. When wine is clear and stable it can be made into a sparkling wine. Follow the directions for Champagne (Chapter 9).

CHAMPAGNE

※

RECIPE 35

1 1-gal. can California White Grape Concentrate
5 cans water
3 lbs. white granulated sugar
3 oz. acid blend
1 level tsp. yeast energizer

5 Campden tablets
½ tsp. grape tannin
1 pkt. Andovin Wine Yeast

Starting specific gravity should be 1.080, acid .70%.

YIELD

6 gallons (30 25-oz. bottles) sparkling white wine.

Mix all ingredients except yeast in primary fermentor. When must is cool (70-75°F.) add yeast. Cover with plastic sheet. Ferment in primary fermentor 6-7 days or until specific gravity is 1.030. Siphon into gallon jugs or carboys and attach fermentation lock. Rack in 3 weeks and again in 3 months. When wine is clear and stable it can be made into a sparkling wine. Follow the directions for Champagne (Chapter 9).

SAUTERNE

❀

RECIPE 36

1 1-gal. can California White Grape Concentrate
5 cans warm water
10 lbs. white granulated sugar
2 8-oz. pkgs. dried bananas
2 oz. acid blend

½ vial yeast energizer
½ tsp. grape tannin
5 Campden tablets
Sauterne yeast

YIELD
6 gallons (30 25-oz. bottles) full-bodied, sweet Sauterne-style wine.

Prepare Sauterne yeast starter according to instructions, 3 days in advance.

Separate bananas and mix all ingredients except wine yeast and 5 lbs. of sugar in primary fermentor. When must is cool (70-75°F.) add yeast. Cover with plastic sheet. Stir gently once a day. When specific gravity is 1.040, withdraw 4 cups of must and dissolve the remaining 5 lbs. of sugar. Stir into primary fermentor. When specific gravity has dropped to 1.030 remove bananas and siphon into gallon jugs or carboy. Attach fermentation locks. Rack when fermentation has stopped. Fine with Serena Wine Finings and sweeten to taste with sugar syrup (2 parts sugar to 1 part water). Add 2 stabilizer tablets per gallon to prevent renewed fermentation.

Age 1 year.

HIDALGO MUSCATEL GRAPE CONCENTRATE

RECIPE 37

1 3-qt. can Mascatel Grape
  Concentrate
4 cans warm water
2½ lbs. white granulated sugar

4 level tsps. acid blend
1 tsp. yeast energizer
3 Campden tablets
Wine yeast

YIELD

3½ gallons (18 25-oz. bottles) full-bodied, strong, slightly sweet dessert wine.

RECIPE 37a

1 3-qt. can Muscatel Grape
  Concentrate
8½ cans (25 qts.) warm water
12 lbs. white granulated sugar
1½ oz. acid blend

3 tsps. yeast energizer
1 tsp. grape tannin
5 Campden tablets
Wine yeast

YIELD

7 gallons (35 25-oz. bottles) light-bodied, strong, sweet dessert wine. Some will prefer this recipe because of its milder muscatel flavour.

Mix all ingredients except wine yeast in primary fermentor. When must is cool (70-75°F.) add yeast. Cover with plastic sheet. Ferment in primary fermentor 6-7 days or until specific gravity is 1.030. Siphon into gallon jugs or carboys and attach fermentation lock. Rack in 3 weeks and again in 3 months. Wine may be sweetened to taste at time of bottling with sugar syrup (2 parts sugar to 1 part water). Add 2 Wine-Art Stabilizer tablets per gallon to prevent renewed fermentation.

Age 1 year.

HIDALGO WHITE GRAPE CONCENTRATE

RECIPE 38

1 3-qt. can White Grape
   Concentrate
4 cans warm water
1 lb. white granulated sugar

1 oz. acid blend
3 Campden tablets
3 tsps. yeast nutrient
½ tsp. grape tannin
Wine yeast

YIELD

3½ gallons (18 25-oz. bottles) dry, full-bodied table wine.

RECIPE 38a

1 3-qt. can White Grape
   Concentrate
8½ cans (25 qts.) warm water
9 lbs. white granulated sugar
3 oz. acid blend

6 Campden tablets
6 level tsps. yeast nutrient
1 level tsp. grape tannin
Wine yeast

YIELD

7 gallons (35 25-oz. bottles) dry, light-bodied table wine.

Mix all ingredients except wine yeast in primary fermentor. When must is cool (70-75°F.) add yeast. Cover with plastic sheet. Ferment in primary fermentor 6-7 days or until specific gravity is 1.030. Siphon into gallon jugs or carboys and attach fermentation lock. Rack in 3 weeks and again in 3 months. Wine may be sweetened to taste at time of bottling with sugar syrup (2 parts sugar to 1 part water). Add 2 Wine-Art Stabilizer tablets per gallon to prevent renewed fermentation.

Age 1 year.

HIDALGO RED GRAPE CONCENTRATE

RECIPE 39

1 3-qt. can Red Grape Concentrate
4 cans warm water
1 lb. white granulated sugar
5 level tsps. acid blend

3 level tsps. yeast nutrient
3 Campden tablets
Wine yeast

YIELD

3½ gallons (18 25-oz. bottles) dry, full-bodied table wine.

RECIPE 39a

1 3-qt. can Red Grape
  Concentrate
8½ cans (25 qts.) warm water
9 lbs. white granulated sugar
2½ oz. acid blend

6 Campden tablets
6 tsps. yeast nutrient
1 tsp. grape tannin
Wine yeast

YIELD

7 gallons (35 25-oz. bottles) dry, light-bodied table wine.

Mix all ingredients except yeast in primary fermentor. When must is cool (70-75°F.) add yeast. Cover with plastic sheet. Ferment in primary fermentor 6-7 days or until specific gravity is 1.030. Siphon into gallon jugs or carboys and attach fermentation lock. Rack in 3 weeks and again in 3 months. Wine may be sweetened to taste at time of bottling with sugar syrup (2 parts sugar to 1 part water). Add 2 Wine-Art Stabilizer tablets per gallon to prevent renewed fermentation.

Age 1 year.

WINE-ART CONCORD GRAPE CONCENTRATE

RECIPE 40

1 1-gal. can Concord Grape Concentrate
8 cans water
14 lbs. white granulated sugar
1 oz. yeast nutrient
5 Campden tablets

1 level tsp. grape tannin
3 level tsps. pectic enzyme powder
2 pkts. Andovin Wine Yeast

YIELD
9 gallons (42 25 oz. bottles) strong, sweet kosher-style wine.

    Mix all ingredients except yeast in primary fermentor. When must is cool (70-75°F.) add yeast. Cover with plastic sheet. Ferment in primary fermentor for 6 days. Siphon into gallon jugs or carboys and attach fermentation locks. Rack in 3 weeks and again in 3 months. When wine is clear and stable, bottle.

    This is not suitable for a dry table wine.

Age 6 months.

GRAPE WINES

※

RECIPE 41. DRY RED TABLE WINE FROM ZINFANDEL

1. Order grapes according to the size of your primary fermentor or fermentors. Remember about 16 lbs. of grapes make 1 gallon of wine, and you should fill the primary fermentor only 4/5 full to allow for expansion.

2. Set the primary fermentor high enough up so that you can siphon from it into the secondary fermentor.

3. Two or three days before delivery of the grapes, prepare the wine yeast starter, about 3% to 5% of the proposed volume of must, using either a Burgundy or an All-purpose wine yeast.

4. Crush the grapes into the fermentor and at once test acid and sugar content. Probably the acid will be too low and the sugar too high. Adjust the acid to .70% by adding acid blend. Adjust the S.G. to 1.095 by adding water if necessary.

5. Immediately add 1 ounce potassium metabisulphite (dissolved in a pint of water) for each 300 lbs. of grapes, and thoroughly stir into the must.

6. Extract 80% to 90% of the stems, if this was not done during the crushing.

7. Check the temperature of the must. It should be 70° to 80°F. If it is over 85°F. cool it with cracked ice tightly tied in a plastic bag. If it is below 65°F. warm the must by suspending in it a plastic pail of hot water (Fig. 15), or by increasing the air temperature of the room.

8. When the temperature is about 75°F. add the yeast starter and cover the fermentor with sheet plastic tied down.

Fig. 15. Raising the temperature of the must.

9. When the cap forms, stir the must at least once a day, to keep the cap broken up and wet. This helps to extract the colour from the skins, and also tends to reduce the risk of spoilage.

10. As the fermentation increases it will produce considerable heat. Cool to 75°F. daily if necessary.

11. When the wine has all the colour and body you want, rack off the free-run wine into secondary fermentors. Here is a rough guide for timing this operation:

    a) 12 hours fermentation gives a deep rosé.
    b) 48 hours gives a light-red wine.
    c) 3 days gives a medium-coloured red wine.
    d) 5 or 6 days gives a dark wine like Chianti.

The hydrometer will also guide you. When the S.G. has fallen 50 degrees, to about 1.045, you will have enough colour for a medium-red wine. For 12 hours before racking, don't stir the wine.

12. If the siphon gets clogged you can pull the plug at the bottom of the primary fermentor (if you are using a barrel) and let the rest of the wine run out through a fairly coarse strainer.

13. If you are only going to make one run of wine from your grapes, use the press at this stage to extract all the wine from the pulp or pomace. If you are going to make "seconds" or "false wine" (see Recipe 45) do not press the pomace.

14. Fill the secondary fermentors only 7/8 full. Keep 15% of the wine apart in gallon jugs or carboys for future topping up. Apply fermentation locks to all secondary fermentors.

15. After 10 to 12 days, rack to eliminate the heavy deposit of yeast and grape solids that tends to cause development of hydrogen sulphide.

16. When fermentation becomes quiet and slow, top up to within an inch of cork or bung and replace fermentation locks. Continue topping up to this level through the following stages.

17. In 3 or 4 weeks, when fermentation is nearly over, rack and sulphite to 60 parts per million (1 Campden tablet per gallon).

18. About the following March, check the S.G. It should be about 0.995 if all the sugar has gone.

19. Fine with gelatin or commercial finings.

20. Ten days later, rack and sulphite again.

That's all the processing this wine needs. Some people start drinking it at this time, when it is about six months old. I would suggest leaving it till fall, then bottling it and leaving it to age for at least a year in bottle. If you have the patience to do this, you'll be rewarded with a much superior wine. If you're in a hurry for something to drink, make some quick-maturing fruit wines and enjoy them while your premium grape wine is aging.

RECIPE 42. DRY RED TABLE WINE FROM HYBRID GRAPES

Try to find hybrid grapes that are known to be non-foxy, and look for 18% to 22% sugar, which hybrids will produce in a good year. But don't worry if they are a little low in sugar. It can always be added.

You will probably find that the must is high in acid, so test it carefully and, if necessary, estimate and add the amount of water required to reduce the acid level to .80%.

After the acid correction, test the S.G. and add enough sugar to give S.G. 1.095 (23% Balling). You must have this proportion of sugar to get the 12% alcohol by volume required for a stable wine.

Otherwise proceed exactly as with Recipe 41, and you will end up with a better wine than you could get from the Zinfandels, especially in a good year.

RECIPE 43. DRY RED TABLE WINE
FROM BLENDED VINIFERAS AND HYBRIDS

Try a 50-50 blend, or else 60% hybrid with 40% *vinifera*. These proportions make an exceptional wine. The high sugar and low acid of the *vinifera* counterbalance the low sugar and high acid of the hybrids.

Test the must, as usual, for acid and sugar content. It should need very little adjustment to arrive at the desired levels of .80% acid and S.G. 1.095.

Some people use as little as 10% of the California *vinifera*. This blend would probably need more correction for acid and sugar. You can experiment with different blends, according to your own taste, or depending on what amounts of the different grapes are available.

For processing, follow Recipe 41.

RECIPE 44. RED WINE FROM CONCORD
OR LABRUSCA GRAPES

Most northern-grown Concords and *labruscas* are very high in acid and very low in sugar compared with *viniferas*. Also, they usually contain pectin, which will keep the wine cloudy unless you add pectinase to remove it.

Proceed as with other grape recipes, testing and correcting acid and sugar levels before starting the fermentation.

If you have no hydrometer or acid-testing kit, you can follow this simple recipe and get tolerable results.

5 lbs. grapes
1 gallon warm water
2½ lbs. granulated sugar
½ tsp. pectic enzyme powder
1 Campden tablet
1 tsp. yeast nutrient
Burgundy or all-purpose wine yeast.

1. Crush the grapes and remove as many stems as you can.

2. Add the remaining ingredients except yeast, stir well to dissolve the sugar and cover the fermentor with sheet plastic.

3. When the must cools to 70°F. add yeast.

4. Stir daily for 7 days. (You have fewer grapes in proportion to the total volume of must than with the preceding grape recipes, so you have to leave the wine on the skins longer to get a good colour.)

5. After 7 days, or when S.G. has falen to 1.040, siphon off the wine through a coarse strainer into a secondary fermentor and apply fermentation lock.

6. In 3 weeks, rack and top up.

7. In 3 months, rack and fine.

8. Ten days after fining, bottle.

9. Age 1 year.

If you want a sweeter wine, add sugar syrup to taste and 2 tablets of wine stablizer and 1 antioxidant tablet per gallon before bottling.

Dry or sweet, this wine can be quite enjoyable for people who like the *labrusca* flavour.

9/17/80 - 1.094   -3gal.   102
9/27/80 - 1.030 - Strained off to Secondary   Bottled 1/27/81
10/80 - Racked   no sugar added
   Rack + Fine 12/28 - Bottle

Do not make false wine from the skins and pulp in this recipe, because you have already exhausted their colour and flavour content.

RECIPE 45. SECOND OR FALSE WINE

Don't be deceived by the name: there's nothing second-rate about this wine. It gives you an excellent wine for the price of the sugar and a little effort, and at least doubles the volume of wine you get from your grapes. Furthermore, it eliminates the work of pressing the pulp and is usually ready to drink in half the time of your first-run wine.

Glance back at Recipe 41, steps 12 and 13. You have drawn off the free-run wine and in the bottom of your primary fermentor lies a mass of skins and pulp mixed with partly-fermented new wine. This is the basis for your second wine. Now proceed as follows:

1. Add to the primary fermentor the same volume of water as the new wine you have just drawn off. Also add, per gallon of water:

2 lbs. sugar
3 tsp. acid blend
1 tsp. yeast nutrient
1/4 tsp. grape tannin

(The pulp is richly laden with yeast, so you don't have to add any more yeast.)

Stir thoroughly and cover.

2. Stir twice a day for 5 to 7 days.

3. When the S.G. has dropped to 1.020 or 1.010 siphon off the new wine into secondary fermentors and continue in exactly the same way as with the first-run wine.

You now have double the wine for an extra 25 cents a gallon!

You can repeat the whole process and get a third run of wine off the same skins. This will have just the same alcoholic content as the first two but will naturally be very thin. Still, there are many people who enjoy a light-bodied wine.

RECIPE 46. WHITE TABLE WINE FROM GRAPES

White wine is not fermented on the pulp or skins of the

grapes. It should be given the minimum contact with air, because oxidation will darken it and make it bitter. Therefore we conduct the entire fermentation in a closed secondary fermentor.

A hot fermentation, too, would tend to increase the oxidation, so it must be kept cool.

Be sure to add an adequate yeast starter to get the fermentation going properly.

1. Order the grapes—either a white grape, or a red-skinned grape known to have white juice.

2. Prepare primary and secondary fermentors before arrival of grapes.

3. As soon as the grapes arrive, crush them. Immediately add 1 ounce metabisulphite crystals for each 350 lbs. of grapes. Dissolve the crystals in a pint of hot water and stir in well.

4. Press the crushed grapes. Let the juice settle 12 hours, then rack off the free-run must into secondary fermentors, three quarters full.

5. Check acid and sugar content. Adjust acid to .70% and S.G. to 1.090 - 1.095.

6. Add the yeast starter, dividing it between the vessels in proportion to the quantity of must in each.

7. Plug the openings of the barrels or carboys with cotton wool to keep out dust and flies. Remember that white wine is often slow to start fermenting, taking perhaps three to five days, especially if temperature is under 70°F. If there is no sign of ferment after 5 days, add more yeast or increase the temperature.

8. Ten to 15 days after onset of the vigorous fermentation, when S.G. has dropped to 1.010, rack and top up. Apply regular fermentation locks. The reserve supply should be kept under a fermentation lock in a vessel just big enough to hold it.

9. After 3 weeks, rack carefully, sulphite to 60 parts per million and top up.

10. Keep in a cool place, well protected from light, and well topped up, till spring.

11. Fine carefully with top-quality commercial finings.

12. If possible, chill the wine for a few days at 32° to 35°F. to precipitate cream of tartar which otherwise might later settle in the bottles.

13. Sulphite to 60 parts per million and bottle.

Light-bodied white table wines are often very good after one year's aging, but usually reach their peak in two years.

There's no need to waste the pulp from this recipe. Use it, *immediately* you have removed the juice, and *without further sulphiting at this stage,* to make a false wine. If it is a red-skinned grape your false wine will be red. Thus you get two kinds of wine from one grape.

RECIPE 47. ROSÉ WINE FROM GRAPE PULP

From the pulp of a white grape you can make rosé false wine by adding a little red wine colouring, or by simply putting it into a barrel that held red wine the previous year.

These are unorthodox ways of making rosé, but they will sometimes yield amazing results.

NOTES ON MAKING SWEET WINES FROM GRAPES

In the past, amateurs have generally made sweet wine by adding sugar until the combination of high alcohol content (16% to 18% by volume) plus residual sugar prevented any further action by the yeast. This method has the advantage of yielding strong wine. But it has two disadvantages: the fermentation is greatly prolonged, and the finished wine takes twice as long to mature as an average table wine. Moreover, in some cases, the resulting wine is very bitter.

With yeast inhibitors based upon sorbic acid we now have a quick, safe and easy way of producing sweet wines. The same basic method can be applied to any wine that you wish to sweeten. Briefly stated, it is:

1. Prepare a dry table wine, about 12% alcohol, from the selected grapes.

2. Sweeten to taste with syrup and add yeast inhibitor, 2 tablets to each gallon.

3. Bottle and age as usual.

After you have gained winemaking experience by following some of the recipes given earlier, you may want to go on and make different kinds of wine from other fruits or combinations of fruits, or from other concentrates.

Here are some principles that will enable you to write your own recipes, with excellent prospects of producing good wine.

Fruit Content

You may have noticed differences between the fruit wine recipes in this book and those published elsewhere. Behind those differences lies an important principle, which will guide you in writing your own recipes.

About four years ago, after much experimentation, I began to suspect that fruit wines were improved by reducing the fruit content in relation to the sugar and water, even to the point of making it necessary to add acid to the must to achieve the desirable level of .65% total acids as tartaric.

In 1965 I went to England by invitation of Grey Owl Laboratories. I discovered that Mrs. S. M. Tritton, M.P.S., F.R.I.C., had been doing considerable research on fruit wines and had arrived at the same conclusion. She had samples of various fruit wines and careful records to prove her point.

On my return to Canada I discussed this matter with the officer in charge of the Federal Department of Agriculture Research Station in Summerland, B.C. He, too, endorsed my conclusions.

I know that most commercial food technologists and oenologists are opposed to this theory of winemaking, but most of them are experienced chiefly in commercial winemaking with *vinifera* grapes. If they have dealt with *labrusca* grapes they have been restricted by the law which, in most winemaking areas, prohibits the amelioration (addition of sugar and water) of any grape or fruit must in excess of 35%. Therefore they have had little incentive for research upon wines of low fruit content, and the concept is still repugnant to them.

But the amateur is not bound by any such law; he is out to get *the best possible wine from his fruit*. High fruit content in such wines as blackberry, apricot, and plum yields a cordial-style wine tasting like heavily sweetened, slightly alcoholic fruit juice, and very readily identifiable with the fruit from which it is made. By contrast, low fruit content—2 to 4 pounds of fruit per gallon—yields a wine in which the basic fruit is not identifiable, which can be mistaken for one made from pure *vinifera* grapes.

So which do you want—a plum wine that tastes like sweet plum-juice mixed with vodka, or a plum wine that tastes like a good commercial grape wine?

If you wish to experiment, make two wines, one using 10 lbs. of prune plums per gallon (plus the necessary other ingredients) and the other using 2½ lbs. of plums per gallon. Taste them both at the end of a year, and judge the difference. Even better, taste them sooner. You will probably find that the wine with the low fruit content is very palatable at six to nine months, while the one with high fruit content will not be drinkable for two to four years.

I strongly recommend, then, that *except for grapes and apples, you use only 2 to 4 pounds of fruit per gallon of wine.*

Sugar Content

There can be no general rules for adding so many pounds of sugar per gallon, because different fruits and concentrates contain different amounts of sugar to start with. The hydrometer will be your guide.

Measure the S.G. of your must, and adjust it according to the kind of wine you wish to make.

Acid Content

Here, too, you should test the must and make the necessary adjustments.

For red grape wines, start with .70% acid.

For white grape wines, start with .75% acid.

For fruit wines, start with .60% acid.

Acid blend, which I recommend in preference to any single acid, consists of equal parts of tartaric, citric and malic acids. One ounce acid blend in 1 gallon of water gives .85% total acids as tartaric.

Yeast

You can generally use an all-purpose wine yeast. If you wish to be more specific, you can use a Burgundy yeast for red table wines, a Steinberg yeast for white table wines and a Champagne yeast for sparkling wines.

If you are not using a ready-to-use yeast, don't fail to make up an ample starter, 3% to 5% of the volume of must.

Yeast Nutrient

For any other than first-run grape wines, some nutrient will be necessary. One level teaspoon per gallon will be about right.

Tannin

First-run grapes, elderberries, black currants and pears contain enough tannin. For other wines add ⅛ to ¼ teaspoon of grape tannin per imperial gallon of must.

Pectinase

This is a valuable additive to all fruits, with the possible exception of the *vinifera* grape (commercial wineries use it even there). It comes in varying strengths up to 50-fold. I recommend ½ teaspoon of 5-fold pectinase per gallon of must.

Metabisulphite

Initial sulphiting of the must requires 120 parts per million. This will be achieved with 2 Campden tablets per gallon. For larger quantities, 1 ounce (4½ tsp.) metabisulphite crystals for 36 gallons of must is the correct proportion.

Recording Recipes

It's a good idea to keep written records of each recipe you make; then, if a batch of wine turns out particularly good, you will be able to make more just like it. A one-two-three process—experiment, record, taste—is an interesting and effective way to develop into a truly creative wine-maker.

CONCLUSION

Following recipes is all very well, but the pleasure of wine-making is heightened when you understand the function of each ingredient and the purpose of each process. Thoughtful reading of the rest of this book, careful observation of your own winemaking procedures, and consultation with other winemakers will give you the necessary insight.

6. Cooperage

The traditional way—and the best way—of aging wine is in barrels. Wine is a living thing and in a barrel it breathes, taking up oxygen through the pores of the wood. From the oak staves and heads, it absorbs the tannin which gives it that desirable tang and bite.

Yet the use and care of white-oak barrels involves a lot of work for the winemaker and a certain amount of risk to the wine. Nowadays even the commercial wineries have given up oak cooperage, except for their premium-quality red table wines.

Big red wines require and deserve storage in oak barrels, but there is no use getting barrels unless you have access to a good cooper. Even with the best of care, barrels sometimes need repairing, and this work requires specialized tools and considerable skill.

BUYING BARRELS

First, don't try to skimp on money. The cost of the best barrels is small compared with the value of the wine they will hold. If you buy cheap barrels, or barrels of doubtful origin, you are simply buying trouble.

The barrel *must be of oak*, and it must have been made and used *only* for the storage of wine, rum, brandy or some other alcoholic beverage. To repeat: don't pick up old barrels of doubtful origin. They may spoil your wine, or even poison you.

Many barrels—those that have contained olives, fish, cherries, orange-base flavouring and such things—have been waxed inside. They are therefore useless as secondary fermentors since for this purpose the porosity of the wood, and the contact of wine with wood, are important. A waxed barrel is no longer porous, so the wine cannot breathe; the wax prevents the wine from touching the wood, so there can be no absorption of tannin. For aging wine, then, the waxed barrel can be no better than, and will probably be inferior to, a glass or plastic container.

Commercial winemakers and distillers use large barrels—forty-gallon capacity for whisky and rum, sixty-gallon for brandy, port, sherry and other wine. A sixty-gallon barrel is too heavy, clumsy and space-consuming for the home winemaker. You will find it more convenient to use barrels from five- to forty-gallon capacity. Buy them from a cooper who specializes in the making and repairing of barrels, and who knows where his used barrels come from.

Here are the dimensions and weights of some common sizes of barrels:

Capacity, gallons	Length, ins.	Diameter, ins.	Weight Empty, lbs.
50	34	26	50
25	26	20	25
15	22	16	15

And here are approximate costs for good-quality reconstructed oak wine barrels:

15 gallons	$17.50
25 "	$19.50
31½ "	$21.00
50 "	$34.00

PREPARING THE BARREL

Reconstructed Barrels

New, unused barrels are hard to obtain in most places. Yours may be a reconstructed barrel, rebuilt from used oak. Then probably one or two staves or ends will be of new oak that has not before been part of a wine barrel. Such new

111

wood is rich in tannin and will give your wine more than the desirable amount of oak flavour.

Here is the standard procedure, used in commercial wineries, to remove excess oak tannin.

1. With water as hot as you can draw it from the tap, make up a solution of 1 pound of soda ash and 2 teaspoons of common household lye to five gallons of water. Make enough to fill your barrel. When you are sure that the ingredients are completely dissolved, pour the solution into the barrel.

2. Let it soak for two or three days.

3. Drain out the solution and flush the barrel three times with clean water.

(If, by chance, you have an all-new, unused oak barrel, repeat these steps at least three times.)

4. Make up a solution of one ounce sodium or potassium metabisulphite and half an ounce citric acid to each gallon of water. One gallon is enough for a five-gallon barrel. Make two or three gallons for bigger barrels. Pour it in, close the bung, and roll the barrel about so that the solution washes repeatedly over every part of the interior.

5. Rinse the barrel once more with clean water, so as not to have too much sulphite or sulphur dioxide in your wine. The barrel is now ready to fill with your new wine.

Old Whisky Barrels

If the barrel has been used for whisky storage, it will have been charred inside. This char must be removed before you put wine in. The cooper will take the barrel apart, scrape off the char, and reassemble it.

Other Used Barrels

Even though a used barrel looks clean and smells sweet, it should be thoroughly cleaned before use. Flush with clean water and treat with metabisulphite solution as described in steps 4 and 5 under the heading "Reconstructed Barrels."

The Spigot

The spigot is a wooden tap that fits into the hole in the barrel-head. Do not put it in before you fill the barrel with wine. The spigot will probably leak during the many months the wine lies in the barrel and the moisture in and around it is a first-class breeding-ground for moulds and vinegar bacteria. Moreover, the spigot tempts people to sample the wine when you are away. Close the spigot-hole with a Number 14, extra-long, premium-quality cork. When it gets wet, the cork will swell, and will be much less likely than a spigot to leak.

Setting Up the Barrel

A barrel used for aging wine or as a secondary fermentor should sit on its side, with the large bung-hole uppermost, and the spigot-hole away from the wall. It should rest on a shaped wooden frame, so that it cannot move and so that, when you are ready to tap off the wine, you can get your bottles under the spigot. If you expect to be racking from barrel to barrel, the first barrel should be set up high enough to let your siphon work.

The frames supporting your barrels (Fig. 16) should be

Fig. 16. Horizontal barrel stands—left, wood; right, angle-iron.

113

of sound lumber, drilled and bolted together (nailing is not good enough), or of angle-iron. A fifty-gallon barrel full of wine weighs four hundred pounds. Do not expect to move it when full.

BARRELS IN USE

Inspection

There is always some evaporation of wine from a barrel; it's called shrinkage. This slight loss is the price we pay for the benefits of oak storage. You dare not let this shrinkage go too far, or a sizeable air-space forms above the wine; and, as we have seen, air is the enemy of wine. So remove the bung and inspect your wine *once a week*. Keep it topped up from a reserve supply of the same wine kept in glass.

Reconstructed or New Barrels

Prior to the first use of a reconstructed or new barrel employ the method described above to remove excess tannin. Then taste the wine after three or four months, to see if it is getting too "oaky," with a bitter, astringent taste like tea that has stood too long on the leaves. If there is any sign of this oaky taste, draw off the wine at once and get it into bottles. To leave it there, absorbing more and more tannin, might make it undrinkable for many years.

As soon as the barrel is empty, give it the soda ash and lye treatment to extract more of the tannin.

But if the wine is satisfactory, let it stay for a full year or more, topping it up weekly.

Drawing Off the Wine

With a sharp knife, slice off the cork in the spigot-hole, flush with the surface of the barrel-head. Place the spigot against the cork. Give the spigot a smart blow with a wooden mallet. This forces the cork into the barrel and simultaneously drives the spigot into the hole. If it is neatly done, scarcely a drop of wine is spilled. See Fig. 17.

Once you tap the barrel, it is best to draw out all the wine at once. To be sure, you hear of Europeans who draw off wine little by little from the barrel. But this is a risky pro-

114

Fig. 17. Barrel used as secondary fermentor, with spigot inserted ready for drawing.

cedure because, as the wine comes out, air must go in, and air carries vinegar bacteria. If you insist on drawing your wine pint by pint, over a period of time, you will very likely have only third-rate, oxidized wine, or even vinegar, left by the time the barrel is half empty.

Some people pour olive oil into the barrel. It forms a film on the surface, and so keeps the air off the wine, but it makes an awful mess of your barrel. Besides, who wants the flavour of olive oil in wine?

You could, if you were careful, keep the top space of the

barrel filled with sulphur dioxide gas. But this is a tricky business, and your wine could easily absorb far more SO_2 than is welcome in a table wine.

The safest and easiest way, therefore, is to tap the barrel, bottle the wine at once or else put it in carboys for bottling in easy stages, and wash the barrel out thoroughly.

Reserve Barrels

A barrel left standing empty will dry out and crack. It may also turn sour or mouldy. To avoid this, use the following procedure:

1. Wash the barrel thoroughly with clean water.

2. Mix up a solution of sodium or potassium metabisulphite, using 2 ounces sulphite crystals to each 5 gallons of water. Make enough solution to fill the barrel.

3. Change the sulphite solution every two months, until you need to use the barrel again for wine.

BARRELS AS PRIMARY FERMENTORS

Used as a primary fermentor, standing upright with one end open, the barrel is simply a convenient container, and neither the porosity nor the tannin content of the oak is significant. So fir or birch barrels will do as well as oak for this purpose. You can buy them from any cooper for less than half the cost of oak.

Whatever wood the primary fermentor is built of, it should be waxed inside before use; the cooper will do this for about a dollar.

Each barrel will require a piece of sheet plastic big enough to be tied over the open end as a cover.

Before putting must into the barrel, rinse it thoroughly with metabisulphite solution, one ounce to the gallon, then with clean water.

When your new wine is transferred to the secondary fermentors, rinse and dry the waxed barrels and store them in a cool place, free from strong odours which might penetrate the wood. It's wise to have the barrels tightened and re-waxed each year, an inexpensive procedure.

Instead of waxing a barrel you can, of course, use it merely as a support for a plastic liner, as suggested in Chapter 2.

BARREL PROBLEMS

Leaks

If you find a barrel leaking, don't try plugging the hole at home. Get the wine out of it into another barrel or into carboys or bottles, and take the leaker back to the cooper. If he has to replace one or more staves, don't forget to treat the barrel with soda ash and lye before you use it again.

Rusting Hoops

This can be serious. If it goes far enough, the barrel falls to pieces and you lose a lot of wine. Take the barrel to the cooper to have new hoops fitted.

As a precautionary measure, paint the outside of your barrels—hoops and all—with boiled linseed oil. This reduces rusting, yet apparently does not inhibit the desirable effects of barrel-aging your wine. The treatment certainly makes your barrels look nice and last longer.

Moulds

You will almost certainly find, at some time, moulds growing around the cork that plugs the spigot-hole, or around the bung at the top of the barrel. They grow from invisible spores which are floating in the air. There is no practicable way of keeping these spores out of the home winery.

Mould must be checked promptly, another argument for weekly inspection. If you neglect mould on the outside of the barrel, it will almost certainly work its way inside, and the slightest bit of mould inside can spoil a whole barrel of wine.

So look closely at the two danger points, cork and bung. If you find mould, treat it promptly. Here are some hints:

1. Sorbate treatment. Make a solution of two wine stabilizer tablets (potassium sorbate) to 4 ounces of water at room temperature. Paint or daub on the mould.

2. Chlorine detergent mix. Dissolve one ounce of the

powder in 8 ounces of hot water and paint or daub on the mould. Do not get this mixture on your hands or into the wine.

3. Commercial mould inhibitors. Carefully carry out the instructions on the package. Do not get these compounds into the wine.

If you do get mould inside a barrel, it must go to the cooper to be taken apart and scraped.

Vinegar

If a partly filled barrel of wine has turned to vinegar, throw out both the liquid and the barrel. There is no safe, certain way of decontaminating barrels impregnated with vinegar bacteria.

CONCLUSION

Despite all these toils and hazards, winemakers still use cooperage. There's something about the look of a row of well-maintained barrels that gladdens the heart of the keen winemaker. There's something special, too, about the wine that comes out of them.

7. Various Operations

Given good ingredients, clean containers and the right temperature, your yeast will dependably produce wine for you. Yet you must do your share by removing by-products from the wine and by getting it safely out of the fermentor and into suitable vessels for aging. Correct bottling technique and storage conditions will further ensure your satisfaction when the time comes to uncork and drink your wine.

RACKING

The purpose of racking is to draw off clear wine while leaving any solid matter undisturbed in the vessel.

In making a batch of wine (except white grape wine) the primary fermentation takes place in contact with the fruit that you are using. During this fermentation, not only is alcohol being formed, but the wine is absorbing flavour and colour from the ingredients.

Yet it would not do to leave the wine there too long, or the pulp would begin to decompose and would produce bad flavours. So as soon as the desired amount of colour and flavour has been extracted the new wine—still fermenting—is racked off the pulp.

A certain amount of suspended matter comes over with the wine and, as the fermentation becomes quieter, begins to settle to the bottom. Even with a white grape wine, there will be some suspended matter. Adding to the sediment is a deposit of yeast cells. The second racking leaves all of this material behind.

Subsequent rackings are mainly to get rid of renewed deposits of yeast. It's inadvisable to leave wine standing too long on its own yeast (except for Champagne yeasts) or a process called autolysis takes place: the yeast starts to feed on itself and imparts bad flavours to the wine.

Racking, then, is a means of purifying and clarifying the wine. A little wine is left behind on the lees each time, but this loss is the price you pay for a clear, tasty, stable wine.

Racking from Primary Fermentor

In the primary fermentor you will find, after a day or two, that a crust or "cap" of fruit pulp is floating on the surface, and that a layer of sediment or "lees" lies at the bottom. When you rack, you want to draw off the clear liquid, the "free-run wine" in between.

During the primary fermentation you have been breaking up the cap twice a day. Before you rack, leave the cap alone for twelve hours, since your task becomes easier if it is fairly firm.

Tie a clean stick on the end of your siphon so that the stick projects an inch or two beyond the end of the tube. The length of projection should be a little greater than the depth of the lees.

Gently insert the end of the tube through the cap. Start siphoning. With the stick you can control the tube as the level of the wine sinks. The projecting stick will prevent the tube from going down into the lees (Fig. 18). You thus avoid the annoyance of carrying blobs of lees over into the secondary fermentor.

At this stage, it is helpful to aerate the wine somewhat. Hold the outlet of the siphon tube against one side of the secondary fermentor, near the top. The wine flows in a film down the inside of the vessel and so receives a gentle exposure to air.

I suggest that the best results will follow from the simple

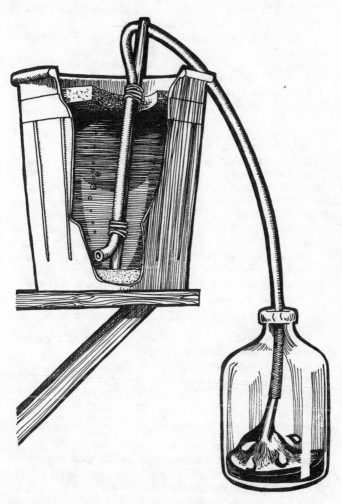

Fig. 18. Racking from primary fermentor.

racking procedure described. Here's a horrible example of trying to do things the complicated way.

Some 20 years ago, I tried to pressure-filter a batch of wine during the first racking. I knew that if I could get enough pressure to push the wine through heavy cloth and a coating of diatomaceous earth, it would be star-bright. I bought 100 feet of plastic hose, placed the wine on the balcony of my second-floor apartment in charge of my wife, and went down to the back yard with a container to receive the wine.

My wife dropped the end of the hose over the balcony and stirred a large quantity of diatomaceous earth into the wine. I started the wine flowing, then quickly clamped a heavy cotton bag to my end of the hose. The gravity drop of 50 or 60 feet produced enormous pressure and the bag gradually expanded like a balloon as the coating of diatomaceous earth and wine solids built up inside it. In a few minutes, it exploded, drenching me with new wine.

My wife was so fascinated by the sight that she forgot to pull her end of the hose out of the primary fermentor. Result—ten gallons of wine lost, and an expensive lesson on how not to filter wine!

Racking From Secondary Fermentor

Here you have no cap to contend with. The stick-and-tube technique avoids picking up the lees.

In all rackings after the first, avoid aerating the wine more than you must. Put the siphon outlet at the bottom of the receiving vessel so that the wine flows out quietly (Fig. 19). Then keep the end of the tube under the surface of the wine.

FINING

Fining is a process used when racking will not clear the wine. Some suspended matter may be too fine to settle to the bottom, or excess pectin may be holding solids in suspension. Whatever the cause of cloudiness, fining will usually get rid of it. As the finings, mixed with the wine, slowly settle to the bottom, they cling to, and draw down with them, the particles of suspended matter.

122

Fig. 19. Racking from secondary fermentor.

Fining with Gelatin

Use one teaspoonful of clear, *unflavoured* gelatin for each 6 gallons of wine in the secondary fermentor. Draw off 1 pint of the wine, soak the gelatin in it for 30 minutes, then heat the liquid to about 180°F. to dissolve the gelatin. Stir this solution thoroughly into the bulk of the wine, replace the fermentation lock and let it stand for 10 days, after which all sediment should be at the bottom. Then rack off the clear wine.

Gelatin will not work unless the wine contains enough tannin to make the gelatin flocculate and settle. Most red-grape wines contain enough tannin. To be sure of success with white

123

wines, add 1/4 tsp. of good-quality grape tannin per gallon, 3 days before fining with gelatin.

Add the same quantity of tannin to fruit wines.

Commercial Finings

Various fining products are sold in winemakers' supply stores under brand names. Each carries instructions for use.

A Warning

Whatever finings you use, don't try to save time by doubling the recommended quantities. Some finings, added in excess, will take the colour out of the wine. Worse, the excess finings may stay in suspension, leaving your wine cloudier than it was before.

MEASURING ALCOHOL CONTENT

Total alcohol content can be measured by an ebullioscope, which costs over $70, or a vinometer, which works tolerably well with dry wines, but not with sweet.

The following method measures the alcohol content by volume of any wine, uses no instrument except the hydrometer, and is as accurate as the ebullioscope. The method, simplified here for amateur use, is based on the researches of William Honneyman, B.Sc., Ph.D., and is described with Dr. Honneyman's kind permission.

1. Measure the S.G. of the wine you wish to test. We will call this figure S.G. 1.

2. Measure exactly one pint of the wine. We will call this the sample.

3. In an enamelled or glass pan, boil the sample down to about half its original volume. This drives off some of the water, but *all* of the alcohol, because alcohol boils at a lower temperature than water. The sample now consists of water, residual sugar, colouring matter, acids and proteins—that is, all the non-alcoholic constituents of the wine.

4. With distilled water or rainwater, make the boiled-down sample up to exactly a pint again. Tap water is not recommended because, in some areas, it has a considerable dissolved mineral content which could affect your results.

5. Cool the sample down to 60°F., or whatever temperature your hydrometer is calibrated for.

6. Read the S.G. of the sample. We will call this reading S.G. 2. You will find it is *higher* than S.G. 1, because you have removed alcohol and replaced it with the same volume of water.

7. Subtract S.G. 1 from S.G. 2. The difference is called the Spirit Indication.

8. Read the alcohol strength from the following table.

Spirit Indication Table

Spirit Indication	Alcohol Strength, % by volume
1.5	1.0
2	1.3
3	2
4	2.7
5	3.4
6	4.1
7	4.9
8	5.6
9	6.4
10	7.2
11	8.0
12	8.8
13	9.7
14	10.5
15	11.4
16	12.3
17	13.2
18	14.1
19	15.1
20	16
21	17
22	18
23	19
24	20
25	21
26	22

As an imaginary example:

    S.G. 1 (S.G. of original wine) = 0.995.

    S.G. 2 (S.G. of sample at stage 6) = 1.011.

    Spirit Indication = 1.011 —0.995 = 16.

    Alcohol strength = 12.3% by volume.

Buy a short-range hydrometer, reading from 0.990 to 1.020. This should let you read S.G. to half a degree. You can then work out a spirit indication to half a unit and, by interpolation on the table, reach a closer value for alcohol strength.

The method as described here lacks some of Dr. Honneyman's refinements, but it yields results close enough for amateur winemakers.

The Pearson Square is used to determine the amount of spirit needed to fortify a wine. It is necessary to know the percentage of alcohol by volume in the spirit to be used for fortification, and also in the wine to be fortified.

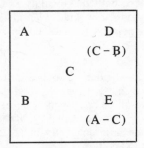

A   Alcohol content of spirit to be used.
B   Alcohol content of wine to be fortified.
C   Desired alcohol content.
D   C minus B. The difference is parts of fortifying spirit required.
E   A minus C. The difference is parts of wine to be fortified.

Example: Suppose the fortifying spirit has a 40% alcohol content, the wine has 15%, and you want to add enough spirit to bring the wine up to 20%.

Subtract B (15) from C (20); the remainder D (5) is parts of spirit to be used in the mixture. Subtract C (20) from A (40); the remainder E (20) is parts of wine to be used.

So you need 5 parts of spirit to 20 parts of wine to bring the mixture up to 20% of alcohol by volume.

The same method can be used to calculate the alcohol content of two wines when blended.

BOTTLING

There's no need to rush your wine into bottles. Early stages of the aging process proceed better in the secondary fermentor than in bottle. Some fruit wines can be bottled after six months, while grape wines can be left in bulk for a year or more while you rack and fine at your leisure.

Some winemakers don't bottle until they need the fermentor for new wine. Once you start to consume a batch of wine, it should certainly be bottled. To empty a large vessel a little at a time risks contamination and oxidation.

Here are a few pointers to make bottling easier.

Choice of Bottles

I recommend the standard 25-ounce bottle. (See Fig. 20, showing traditional shapes.) Bear in mind that when a bottle is opened it should all be consumed at once. Remember, too, that if guests are present they will stay till the bottle is empty no matter how much it holds. So don't tempt them with half-gallon and gallon bottles.

Fig. 20. Traditional bottle shapes: left to right, Burgundy, Claret or Sauterne, Rhine, Sherry or Port.

Try to find sound bottles designed to hold wine. It may be imagination, but many people don't enjoy wine so much if they suspect that the bottle previously held whisky, ammonia or disinfectant. You may have to buy wine bottles if the law in your area requires bartenders to destroy empties.

The bottles for your premium table wines should be designed for corking. Screw-top bottles will do for fruit wines and sweet wines.

Red and rosé wines should be bottled in brown or green glass, to shield them from light which would fade the wine. White wines may go in clear bottles, though some people use coloured bottles for these, too, as a precaution.

Cleaning Bottles

Whether your bottles are new or second-hand, clean them before you fill them.

Don't sterilize bottles by putting them in the oven. The heat shortens the life of any bottle, and gravely heightens the risk of explosions with sparkling wines. Carefully treated, good bottles can be used many times.

A safe method of cleaning is to soak the bottles in a hot solution of chlorinated detergent or of quaternary ammonium bactericide. Chlorinated detergent is the best thing for removing labels and all types of dirt or mould from used bottles.

Remove every trace of sterilant by rinsing. If you are handling a lot of bottles, you'll find that a bottle-washer (Fig. 21) fixed on your tap saves water and work.

Filling the Bottles

For quantities up to 10 gallons, the siphon tube, 1/4-inch or 3/8-inch bore, is sufficient equipment. If you wish, you can get for about $2 a bottle-filler attachment (Fig. 22) for the siphon that makes the job easier and avoids spilling. Or you can get a siphon with a shut-off valve at the outlet for $6 to $8.

With wine in a barrel, you need only spigot and funnel for easy bottling.

Twenty or more gallons of wine is too much for one person to put into 25-ounce bottles at one session. Empty the barrel into carboys first, for final bottling in easy stages.

Wine should be between 60° and 70°F. for bottling. Re-

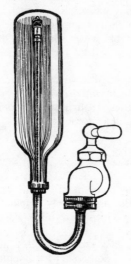

Fig. 21. Spray bottle washer.   Fig. 22. Stop-start bottle filler.

member not to fill bottles to the brim. Leave room for corks to go in.

Antioxidants

In most cases, some form of antioxidant is necessary at the time of bottling. Sulphur dioxide usually serves the purpose very well.

Dissolve 1 ounce of metabisulphite crystals in 1 gallon of water. Rinse each bottle with this solution, then drain well. The amount of solution clinging to the bottle adds about 50 parts per million of SO_2 to the wine. This is cheaper than using Campden tablets.

Antioxidant tablets contain ascorbic acid (vitamin C), an antioxidant that does not add SO_2 to the wine. They are sometimes used in conjunction with Campden tablets. The two seem to reinforce each other.

If you are sensitive to the smell of SO_2 and feel that you have already added enough of it to your wine, then antioxidant or vitamin C would be the best thing to use when bottling. Follow instructions on the package. Don't add too much, or normal bottle aging will be retarded.

Bottling Sweet Wines

Be absolutely sure that your sweet wine is stable, that it is not fermenting, and will not start fermenting again if it happens to be warmed by a few degrees. If wine resumes fermentation inside a screw-capped bottle, the bottle will explode.

If you have any doubts, add 200 to 300 parts per million of wine stabilizer, usually packaged as potassium sorbate tablets, which will prevent the growth of any yeast that may be present.

CLOSURES

Wine corks are cylindrical, unlike medicine bottle corks which are tapered. For an airtight, leakproof closure, the cork must be bigger than the bottleneck into which it fits. A cork that slides in easily is useless. Don't try pushing corks in by hand, by jamming the bottle against a door-post, or by hitting the cork with a hammer. Get a corker, a gadget that compresses the cork and inserts it. Corkers (Fig. 23) come in various models, hand-held and table-mounted.

Corks come from Spain and Portugal, so are measured in millimeters. Lengths vary from 38 to 50 mm., diameters from 22 to 24 mm. I recommend using 22.5 by 40 mm. corks for the standard 25-ounce bottle.

To prepare non-waxed corks for use, soak them for 20 minutes in a weak sulphite solution, 1 ounce of stock solution to 1 pint of warm water. (The stock solution consists of 2 ounces of sulphite per gallon or water.) This softens and sterilizes the corks.

Waxed corks are more difficult for amateurs, but can be used if you have a good metal corker and apply a little vegetable oil to the slot or teeth of the machine for every five or six corks, to stop the wax from sticking to the metal. Waxed corks should not be soaked before use.

Don't try to salvage old corks and screw-caps. New ones

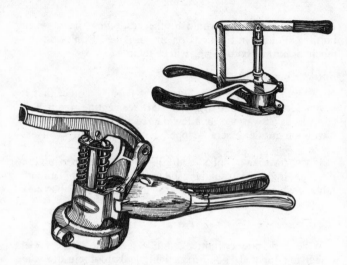

Fig. 23. French-made (top) and Italian-made (bottom) corking
implements.

are cheap enough, and worth the added protection. Plastic
stoppers, though not so elegant as corks, are re-usable, and
perhaps most economical in the long run. To clean plastic
stoppers for re-use, wash them in stock sulphite solution.

A refinement you may like to use for your best wines is
to apply capsules of viscose, lead or aluminum over the
corks. You can get the capsules, with instructions for use,
where you buy your corks.

Fig. 24 shows different methods of bottle closure.

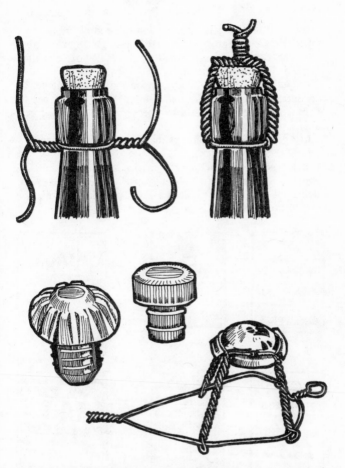

Fig. 24. Top: An economical method of wiring down corks or plastic champagne stoppers, using 2 pieces of No. 20 copper wire, 10″ long. Just as effective, but not as expensive, as regular champagne wires. Bottom: Left to right, plastic stopper for champagne bottle, plastic stopper for ordinary bottle, capsule to wire over champagne cork.

LABELLING

Accurate labelling is essential for the conscientious wine-maker. Here's the information that should go on every label:

1. The type of wine: Dry Red, Sweet White, Sparkling White, or your own variation.

2. The ingredients: For grapes use the varietal name; for concentrates, country of origin, brand name and type; for other fruits, the ingredients by species (and variety if relevant).

3. Age of the wine, date of making, date of bottling.

4. Maker's name.

Blank gummed labels, with spaces for information, are available at nominal cost. Many creative winemakers, producing on a large scale, design their own labels and have them printed. (See Fig. 25.)

Fig. 25. Typical label designs.

There is always some risk of losing wine in barrels, carboys, or even gallon jugs. But you seldom lose wine if it is sound when bottled, and if it has a new closure, properly applied.

Lay corked bottles on their sides. The wine keeps the cork moist and prevents it from shrinking and admitting air. The safest storage is in a rack that gives each bottle a compartment to itself, allowing you to withdraw any bottle without jogging the others. Screw-top bottles should be stored upright. See Figs. 26 and 27 for various storage racks.

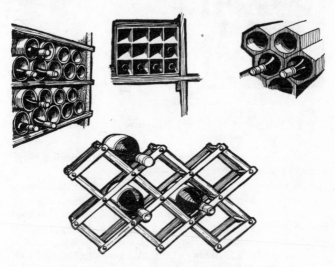

Fig. 26. Storage racks. Top, left to right: Using 48-oz. juice tins, or cardboard mailers; cardboard wine case with dividers; drain tiles. Bottom: Collapsible rack.

Here are four general principles for storage of all wines:

1. Even temperature. A few degrees' difference between summer and winter won't do harm, provided the change occurs slowly and steadily. What damages wine is rapid and frequent heating and cooling. Use your ingenuity to find

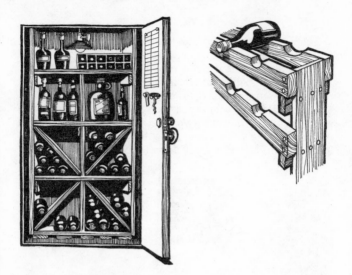

Fig. 27. Left, closet cellar, with honeycomb bins; right, closet rack.

places in your home that have a steady temperature. Under-ground storage is best.

2. Clean, pure air. It's a matter of opinion whether smells can get into a bottle. They can certainly get into a barrel, and they can contaminate the neck of a wine-bottle so that the wine picks up the odour as it is poured. So don't expose your wine to rotting garbage, rubber tires, paint, gasoline, coal oil, ammonia, or any other strong-smelling substances.

3. Steadiness. Vibration is an enemy to aging wine. If your bottles get a good shaking every time you climb the stairs, the wine cannot age properly.

4. Patience. Allow ample time for bottle-aging, to get the truly remarkable benefits of the process. The wine should lie in bottle at least as long as it lay in the secondary fermentor. It is doubtful whether any wine worthy of the name is near its peak in less than a year. Most wines keep improving up to 18 months or two years. Red wines need longer aging

than white, and the stronger a wine is, the longer it should be aged. Remember, bouquet only develops in the bottle.

OPENING

Many connoisseurs contend that red table wines, especially Burgundies, should be opened and exposed to the air for several hours before serving. This is not necessary with modern wines which contain no excess sulphur dioxide. The idea may have started in England, where wine was stored in very cool cellars, and was brought to room temperature—about 68°F.—before being served.

Some people find difficulty in using the plain T-shaped corkscrew. Uncorking is easier with a lever-action corkscrew, which spares you all the tugging, and extracts the cork smoothly by pressure against the bottle-neck.

A favourite cork extractor with many is a hypodermic needle that penetrates the cork and pumps air beneath it. The cork is forced out gently, with no risk of having broken pieces of cork fall into the wine. (This extractor should never be used on Chianti bottles or square liquor bottles which might not stand the internal pressure.) See Fig. 28 for 3 types of cork extractors.

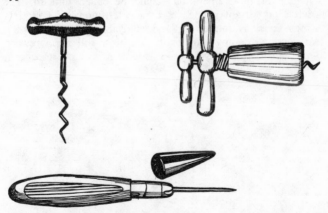

Fig. 28. Top left, traditional T-style corkscrew; top right, wooden cork puller with counter-screw; bottom, hypodermic cork extractor.

PREPARING WINE FOR COMPETITION

Here are some hints that will help you make the best possible presentation of your wines if you enter a contest.

1. Bottle. Although the wine may have been aged in a coloured bottle, it must be exhibited in a clear one, so that the judge can see its colour. Rebottle a month in advance, to give the wine time to settle down in its new quarters. Fill nearly to the top and keep in a completely dark place.

2. Closure. Either corks or screw caps are usually acceptable.

3. Labels. There must be a stick-on label identifying the type, ingredients and age of the wine. In many contests the maker's name must be on a separate, tie-on label, so that it can be removed before the judge sees the bottle.

These are general principles. If there are special local rules, obey them carefully. Presentation counts for only a small part of the total score, but one or two points lost here can make the difference between winning a prize and being an also-ran.

CONCLUSION

None of these operations could be called difficult. Yet each is important and each, by the testimony of countless winemakers, is interesting and enjoyable. There's a keen satisfaction in doing a job right. Your wine will amply reward you for every effort you make to give it correct, respectful, loving treatment.

8. Common Problems

Let's discuss a few problems that winemakers sometimes encounter, with suggestions for prevention or cure.

STUCK FERMENT

Occasionally a batch of wine will stop fermenting too soon, before all the sugar has been consumed and before the yeast has reached its level of alcohol tolerance. Bubbles stop rising through the must and through the fermentation lock when you know that the ferment should have continued days or weeks longer. A quick check with the hydrometer will confirm the situation: the S.G. has not fallen as low as it should with a completed ferment.

Here are the most common causes of "stuck ferment," and the appropriate remedies.

1. Too low a temperature for the wine yeast you are using. Many yeasts cannot function properly below 60°F.

Cure: Warm the must to 70° or 75°F. and see if that revives the fermentation.

2. Too high a temperature. If the primary fermentation was allowed to go above 85°F. (as a large-volume must may easily do in hot weather) the yeast could be seriously weakened.

Cure: Using a fresh yeast starter, ferment the must again. Proceed as follows:

a) Prepare a cup of good, strong yeast starter, with the same kind of yeast that you used in the initial fermentation.

b) Draw off a pint of the wine and mix it with the starter. Keep it at 70°F. in a separate vessel until it begins to ferment.

c) Draw off a quart of the stuck wine, mix with the pint, and keep it apart till it is all fermenting.

d) Draw off a gallon of wine, mix with the 3 pints and keep it apart till it is all fermenting.

e) Continue adding the stuck wine in progressively larger doses to the portion that you have reactivated, till the whole must is fermenting.

3. Insufficient nutrient. Musts made from some fruits (peaches and blueberries for example), will not support a strong, complete fermentation without addition of proper nutrients.

Cure: Add a small amount of yeast energizer. If this revives the fermentation, see that the must does not heat up above 75°F.

4. Badly balanced recipe—too much sugar, for example, giving a S.G. over 1.120. Remember that excess sugar, like excess alcohol, will inhibit yeast action.

Cure: Dilute the must with water and acid—about 1 gallon of water and 1 ounce of acid blend for each 5 to 8 gallons of must. If none of the other causes is operative, this will usually restart the fermentation and carry it through to completion.

AUTOLYSIS

Yeast cells still alive in the wine during secondary fermentation begin to feed on the lees. This produces bad flavours in the wine.

Cure: Systematic racking. Don't let wine stand too long on sediment.

FLOWERS OF WINE (MYCODERMA)

A yeast-like organism forms a film on the surface of wine exposed to air. Small islets form at first, then coalesce to cover the surface of the wine. Mycoderma oxidizes the alcohol to CO_2 and water, forming by-products that include acetic acid.

Once the mycoderma has completely covered the surface of your wine the resulting bad flavour cannot be removed or disguised. Throw out the wine.

Cure: If you detect mycoderma early enough, by noticing the first few islets and the first traces of a sour, vinegary smell, proceed as follows to eliminate the bad flavour and save the wine:

1. Strain the wine through close-woven cloth to remove all particles of mycoderma.

2. Sulphite with 2 Campden tablets per gallon.

3. Bottle immediately.

4. Thoroughly disinfect the fermentor in which the mycoderma appeared.

Prevention: Mycoderma *must have air,* so you can prevent its appearance by excluding air from your wine during secondary fermentation and aging.

EXPLODING BOTTLES

Danger! If *one* bottle from a batch of wine explodes, there is a grave risk that others may follow. To avoid this danger, select the probable cause from the list below and apply the cure.

1. Bottling before secondary fermentation is finished.

Cure: Open the bottles and return the wine to carboys or barrels under fermentation locks until fermentation is complete, with the S.G. steady for one month below 1.000. Then rack, sulphite and rebottle.

2. Failure to stabilize sweetened wines.

Cure: Same as for 1 above. Note that potassium sorbate, or other stabilizers, *will not stop fermentation*: they can only *prevent it restarting* once it has stopped.

3. Wrong type of bottle for sparkling wines.

Cure: Uncork all bottles of the batch, let the gas escape, and rebottle as a still wine.

4. Excessive sweetening of sparkling wines.

Cure: Same as for #3 above.

5. One defective bottle in a batch of proper Champagne bottles.

Prevention: Next time, tap bottles briskly together by pairs before use. This will often reveal flaws in the glass that might escape visual inspection.

VINEGAR SMELL AND TASTE

This is sometimes called "sour wine." Vinegar yeast of one sort or another is almost omnipresent, but it needs oxygen to convert alcohol to acetic acid. So you have this problem because fermentation locks were not applied soon enough, or secondary fermentors were not topped up.

No Cure! It's as easy to turn lead into gold as to turn vinegar into wine. So if you smell or taste vinegar in your wine, throw it away. (Don't bother saving it for salads. Wild vinegar yeasts do not make good vinegar.) Carboys or bottles that have contained vinegary wine should be thoroughly sterilized.

Prevention: If one bottle or carboy of wine has gone to vinegar, try to find out how it happened, and check the rest of your wine to see if any more is contaminated, or to take precautions against such contamination. In detecting vinegar spoilage your nose is your best guide; the vinegar smell is unmistakable.

ROTTEN-EGG ODOUR

The rotten-egg smell is caused by hydrogen sulphide gas, H_2S. It often develops in wine made by amateurs, particularly in musts made of California *vinifera* grapes that are very ripe, low in acid, and have been sprayed with copper sulphate to prevent mildew. Free sulphur, trapped in the lees of new wine, is readily reduced to hydrogen sulphide, and the unforgettable smell begins to rise from the wine.

Cure: If you catch this problem early, you can usually cure it. Rack the wine, splashing it vigorously in the process to get it well aerated. (This is an exception to our usual rule for racking.) Add 1 Campden tablet per gallon.

Repeat the procedure, if need be, three or four times over a period of 6 to 9 months, to eliminate the unpleasant smell.

If this does not work, you might try baking the wine to make Madeira or American-style Sherry (see Chapter 9). Baking will drive off all sulphur odours.

Prevention: You can usually prevent this unpleasant development by early racking from the secondary fermentor, even though the wine is still fermenting. Rack 10 days after putting the wine in the secondary fermentor, and rack again as soon as fermentation appears complete, in 6 to 8 weeks.

Sulphiting (1 Campden tablet per gallon) at the second racking will help guard against subsequent development of hydrogen sulphide.

MUSTY SMELL

A musty smell in a newly opened bottle of wine may be due to fungus or mould growth on or in the cork. Examine the cork closely, breaking it up, if need be, to look inside any cracks or holes. If you find fungus or mould, check your other bottles to see if it is spreading.

Cure: Draw mouldy corks, sterilize the bottle-necks by wiping with a cloth dipped in sulphite solution, and recork with clean, sterilized corks.

Prevention: Use only new corks and sulphite them properly before use. Discard any cork that has big cracks or cavities. Eliminate dampness in the wine storage area.

BOTTLE STINK

A sulphurous stench noticeable on opening bottled wine is caused by excessive use of SO_2 at the time of bottling or during the secondary fermentation.

Cure: Leave the bottle standing uncorked for a few hours and the smell may pass off. Decanting the wine will speed the process.

YEASTY FLAVOUR

A yeasty taste may be caused by use of the wrong yeast, by insufficient racking and fining, or by drinking the wine too new. There is no cure.

Prevention: Be more careful with the next batch of wine, and leave the rest of this batch alone until it is properly aged.

OXIDATION

In Sherries and Madeiras a slightly oxidized flavour is

143

acceptable; practically all other wines are distasteful if they become oxidized. Oxidized wine is brown in colour and tends to be bitter. Wines made from over-ripe fruit have excessive oxydase enzyme and low acid content. They are particularly apt to oxidize.

There is no cure for an oxidized wine.

Prevention: 1. Check the acid balance of your must and correct if necessary.

2. Ferment at the proper temperature, within the range of 60° to 80°F.

3. Sulphite the must and wine with one Campden tablet per gallon.

4. Once the primary fermentation is over, exclude air from the wine.

CONCLUSION

Most of the incurable problems encountered by amateur winemakers are caused by excessive exposure of wine to air. Many defects can be cured if caught in time. So two useful rules are:

1. Keep air off your wine.

2. Regularly inspect your wine, with eye and nose.

9. Three Special Wines

When you have gained some experience with the techniques and recipes in the preceding chapters, you may like to try your hand at the more complicated processes which will produce Flor Sherry, Madeira and Sparkling Wines.

FLOR SHERRY

Authentic Sherry is produced from Palomino, Pedro Ximenez and Muscatel grapes grown in the neighbourhood of the town of Jerez in Spain. "Sherry," in fact, is a mispronunciation of Jerez.

Sherry is a blended wine. Each shipper maintains a "solera," a stock of Sherries of various ages, and blends year after year so as to produce a finished wine of constant quality. So Sherry has none of the fluctuations from good to fair to indifferent that occur when wines are made solely from one year's vintage.

Sherry is unique among wines in that, while maturing, it is deliberately exposed to air. You have read repeated warnings about keeping air away from a wine—particularly a white wine—once the primary fermentation is over. With Sherry, however, we depend on some degree of oxidation to produce the typical colour and flavour.

The flavour of top-quality sherries is also due in part to a film of yeast, called the "flor," which, in the presence of oxygen, grows on the surface of the wine. To produce this flor you should use a special flor yeast. Ordinary Sherry yeast is unlikely to yield a flor.

The operation of the flor yeast can be seen if you ferment in a glass vessel. Some weeks after the start of fermentation the yeast begins to climb the sides of the secondary fermentor, eventually reaching the surface. At first it looks like little floating islands, then the islands unite to form an unbroken film. Eventually the film thickens and becomes wrinkled. As the weeks pass, the wine beneath the flor becomes lighter in colour.

Successful flor formation (with subsequent lightening of the wine) produces the highest quality dry Sherry, named Fino.

Other kinds of Sherry, not produced under the flor, are Amontillado, a medium-light, dry wine, and Oloroso, which is dark brown, sweetened, and of high alcoholic content.

Attempt a Fino Sherry first. If the flor fails to form, you will have an Oloroso, which is still a first-class wine in its own right.

Here is a recipe for 5 gallons of Fino Sherry using California white grape concentrate.

1 1-gal. can White Grape Concentrate	3 tsps. yeast nutrient
4½ cans water	½ tsp. yeast energizer
5 lbs. white granulated sugar	2 tsps. grape tannin
1 oz. tartaric acid	Sherry Flor yeast
3 Campden tablets	6 oz. gypsum
	Additional 5 lbs. of sugar

The risky part of Sherry making is the period when it is exposed to oxygen, because you may possibly get contamination and lose your wine. But if you are careful about cleanliness of all utensils, and if you make a good, strong yeast starter, you should have no trouble.

This recipe for Sherry Flor is based on what we know about the production of Spanish Sherry. In Spain the barrels of wine are exposed to the heat of the day and the coolness of night. This fluctuation in temperature seems to play an important part in the production of a flor. In the home an ideal place can be near a furnace. When the furnace is firing, the temperature might go up to 80°. But at night time, or on a warm day when the furnace is not firing so frequently, the temperature may be as low as 60°.

Use gallon jugs for secondary fermentors; the small bulk of liquid allows easier heat transfer. For this recipe, you will need 7 gallon jugs, to allow plenty of air space above the wine. Here's the process, step by step.

1. Prepare the Sherry Flor yeast culture several days in advance.

2. Mix all ingredients except gypsum, yeast, and the 5 lbs. extra sugar.

3. Check S.G. of must. It should be 1.100.

4. Take 2 cups of prepared must and put aside.

5. Add three-quarters of the active yeast starter to the must in the fermentor. Then take the two cups of must you put aside, and add to the remaining yeast starter in the bottle. This is the "booster starter" which you will use later.

6. Cover the fermentor with a plastic sheet and keep in a warm place (70-75°F.).

7. Fermentation should start in two days; then add the booster starter, the additional 5 lbs. of sugar, and stir vigorously to aerate.

8. Allow to ferment 6 days in the primary fermentor, stirring twice a day.

9. Put ½ ounce of gypsum in each gallon jug; siphon wine into the jugs, leaving each jug 2/3 full.

10. Attach fermentation locks, but do not put liquid in the lock as you usually do.

11. In two weeks, siphon each gallon of wine on to ½ ounce gypsum and 1 ounce sugar. Do not stir the sugar in. Leave the jugs 2/3 full. Attach fermentation locks again. This time put water in the locks.

12. Within 2 months, flor should appear as small, white floating islands. If all goes well, the flor makes a complete, thick layer on the surface.

13. Leave the jugs undisturbed for 6 to 9 months until the wine acquires the Fino color and flavor. Any vibration will cause the flor to drop prematurely. Eventually, the flor will drop on its own. When this happens, immediately rack the wine into clean jugs, top up and apply screw caps.

14. The wine can now be fortified with brandy and bottled. It should be allowed to age for a year.

If the flor does not form, you end up with an Oloroso Sherry. This should be sweetened on bottling. Don't skimp the syrup; some commercial Olorosos have 10% to 12% residual sugar.

Flor Sherry—Continuous Production

The method described above produces a single batch of wine. After racking (Step 13), the flor is thrown down the drain.

By the following method, if you use a carboy instead of gallon jugs, you can keep the flor unbroken as long as you wish and use it to produce batch after batch of Fino Sherry. The secondary fermentor is fitted with input and outlet tubes (see Fig. 29). When the first batch of wine has acquired the Fino quality you draw off *only a part of it*. As the level of wine falls, the flor sinks, but remains unbroken. Then, through the input tube, you introduce enough new wine (made from the same recipe in a separate fermentor) to raise the flor to its former level. In another month or two you draw off more Fino, replenish the fermentor with more new wine, and so on indefinitely.

Here is a detailed description of the procedure:

1. Make the initial batch of wine exactly as before, but when the primary fermentation is over, rack carefully to remove all sediment. This means that the flor will be slower in forming but, since it is going to remain in place for a long time, we must be sure that there is not the slightest scrap of pulp material beneath it. Any such pulp, in the long run, would start decaying and spoil the flavour of the wine.

2. Place the clear wine in the secondary fermentor fitted up according to the diagram. Keep it at 60° to 65°F. and wait for the flor to form.

3. About 4 months after starting the first batch of wine, prepare a second batch in another fermentor. This wine should be fermented down to S.G. 1.010 or less by the time it is introduced under the flor.

148

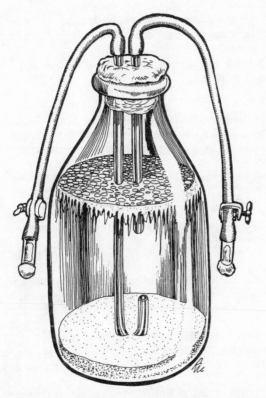

Fig. 29. Secondary fermentor for continuous production of Flor Sherry. The mouth of the fermentor is plugged with cotton wool, as are the ends of the siphon (left) and the input tube.

4. Three to 6 months after the flor has covered the main batch, draw off about one third of the Fino wine (about 10 bottles), fine it if necessary, and add 2 ounces of brandy per bottle.

5. Replace it with the same volume of wine from the second batch.

6. When the colour change shows that the new wine has been transformed to Fino, draw off another 10 bottles and replenish again.

7. Continue the process, making fresh batches of replacement wine as required.

Flor Sherry from Fruit

Grape concentrate yields the best Flor Sherry, but if you use a high-quality Flor Sherry yeast, you can get quite acceptable results from other fruits. The following recipe makes 5 gallons.

8 lbs. plums *or*	4 gallons hot water
8 lbs. greengages *or*	2½ tsp. yeast energizer
8 lbs. apples	2½ tsp. yeast nutrient
8 lbs. raisins (light colour)	2 oz. acid blend
150 oz. sugar syrup	2 tsp. pectic enzyme powder
1¼ tsp. grape tannin	Grey Owl Sherry Flor yeast

(To be perfectly clear, you use *one* of the first three fruits listed, *plus* the raisins.)

1. Mash the fruit thoroughly and cover with boiling water.

2. When the must has cooled, add as much of the sugar syrup as is necessary to bring the starting gravity precisely to 1.115.

3. Add the other ingredients and ferment at 70° to 75°F.

4. When the vigorous primary fermentation is over, rack to get rid of the pulp, then proceed as with the grape concentrate.

You can also use raisins or sultanas alone, if you wish. In that case, use 2 lbs. of raisins or sultanas per gallon of must.

MADEIRA

Madeira is an excellent aperitif or after-dinner wine for amateurs. You should have no difficulty in making something quite comparable to a high-grade commercial Madeira.

Real Madeira, from the island of that name, gains its distinctive flavour from a "cooking" process. The fully fermented wine is placed in a room called the *estufa* which is slowly warmed to about 140°F., held there for 3 or 4 months, then slowly cooled to about 70°F.

The wine is partially bleached with bone charcoal and fined up to five times for perfect clarity. Some Madeiras are sweetened with grape concentrate.

Fig. 30. A simple *estufa* (cutaway view).

There are four types of Madeiras, ranging from very dry to sweet. The dryest is called Sercial, a pale wine about the colour of Amontillado that needs 8 to 10 years' aging. Verdelho is medium-dry and is slightly cheaper than Sercial. Bual is medium-sweet, and Malmsey is a heavy dessert wine.

Madeira is the longest-lived of wines. If the corks are changed every 20 years, it has been known to live 150 years.

A few North American wineries are copying Madeira, and in fact nearly all American Sherry is made by a Madeira-type cooking process.

A home-made *estufa* is shown in Fig. 30. To make it, you will need:

1. A cardboard box or a tea chest.

2. Either bricks or short pieces of 2 x 4 to put under the secondary fermentor (glass carboy or oak barrel).

3. Aluminum foil to line the box.

4. A light on an extension cord, such as used by auto mechanics, with a metal cage around the bulb.

5. Thermometer.

6. Blanket to retain heat.

You may have to experiment with different light bulbs to get the correct temperature, 110-125°F. Start with a 60-watt bulb. If the temperature is below 110°, increase to 100-watt; if over 125°, drop to 40-watt. If you are using a cardboard box, take care to avoid fire hazard.

If you do not wish to make an *estufa,* here are some alternate methods of cooking your Madeira:

a) Place a small heating pad under the barrel and leave it on low.

b) Insert a thermostat-controlled aquarium heater in the barrel or carboy.

c) Put the barrel in the warmest corner of a heated greenhouse.

MADEIRA RECIPE 1. BUAL OR MALMSEY MADEIRA

        80 oz. white grape concentrate
        80 oz. fig concentrate
        24 oz. dried bananas
        9 gallons hot water
        10 Campden tablets
        5 oz. acid blend
        3 tsp. yeast energizer
        3 tsp. yeast nutrient
        80 oz. Madeira or Sherry wine yeast starter
        Sugar syrup

This recipe will yield 12 gallons of finished wine.

1. Mix all ingredients except yeast and syrup in a 13- or 14-gallon primary fermentor. Hot water helps soften the dried bananas.

2. When the must cools to 70°F. add sufficient syrup to raise S.G. to 1.100. Add yeast and cover the fermentor with cheesecloth.

3. When fermentation subsides, rack into secondary fermentor. Apply fermentation lock full of cotton wool. (There is no need to keep this wine topped up.)

4. After a week read S.G. If it is 1.000 or less, add syrup to raise it to 1.010, *but no higher*. Replace fermentation lock.

5. Test S.G. weekly. Every time it falls to 1.000, raise it to 1.010 with syrup. You may be able to do this 5 or 6 times over a few months.

6. When S.G. holds steady for a month, you have about 18% alcohol. Sweeten again to 1.010.

7. Cook the wine for 3 or 4 months, either in oak or in glass. If possible maintain a steady temperature of 130°F. If the temperature is lower, the wine will take longer to mature.

8. After cooking, fine and bottle. 1 or 2 ounces of brandy added to each bottle (optional) will improve the wine.

9. Age 1 or 2 years.

For those who like Madeira or Sherry, the above is the best recipe in the book!

MADEIRA RECIPE 2. QUICK MADEIRA

You can make a Madeira-type wine in 3 to 4 months, using American white grape concentrate and American Sherry flavour concentrate. I call the wine Madeira because the American Sherry is made by a cooking process. The flavour concentrate is the de-alcoholized wine concentrated 8 to 1, and is much like Madeira in flavour and bouquet. The recipe makes 5 gallons.

    1 gallon white grape concentrate
    4 gallons hot water
    2 oz. acid blend
    1 tsp. grape tannin
    3 tsp. yeast nutrient
    1 tsp. yeast energizer
    5 lbs. granulated sugar
    4 cups all-purpose wine yeast starter

1. Mix all ingredients except yeast in a 7-gallon primary fermentor.

2. When must cools to 70°F., add yeast.

3. In 5 to 7 days, rack into secondary fermentor and attach fermentation lock.

4. Rack again in 3 or 4 weeks, or sooner if ferment appears complete. Keep topped up.

5. In 3 months, wine should be clear and stable. Rack off any slight remaining deposit.

6. Add 3 stabilizer tablets (potassium sorbate) per gallon, 6 to 8 ounces standard sugar syrup per gallon, and American Sherry wine flavour concentrate to taste.

7. Bottle, adding 1 or 2 ounces brandy per bottle.

8. Age 1 or 2 months.

This easily made wine will delight anyone who enjoys Madeira and American Sherry.

MADEIRA RECIPE 3. PRUNE PLUM MADEIRA

This is a one-gallon unit; multiply as many times as you wish.

3 lbs. Italian prune plums, destoned
1 lb. raisins, chopped or coarse-ground
1 gallon hot water
2½ lbs. cane sugar
2 Campden tablets
1 tsp. yeast nutrient
¼ tsp. grape tannin
1 tsp. acid blend
½ tsp. pectic enzyme powder
1 cup Madeira wine yeast starter

1. Mix all ingredients except pectic enzyme and yeast.
2. When must cools to 70°F. add pectic enzyme and yeast.
3. Ferment on the pulp for 7 days, then pour through a coarse strainer into a secondary fermentor and apply fermentation lock.
4. In 3 or 4 weeks rack and read S.G.
5. Proceed with syrup feeding as in the first Madeira recipe: every time S.G. falls to 1.000 add syrup to raise it to 1.010.
6. When fermentation ceases and S.G. remains steady for 1 month, cook in the *estufa* for 3 months.
7. Fine, fortify and sweeten to taste.
8. Age 1 to 2 years in bottle.

MADEIRA RECIPE 4. RAISIN MADEIRA

To make one gallon:

    4 lbs. raisins, chopped or coarse-ground
    2 lbs. sugar
    1 imperial gallon hot water
    ¾ oz. (5 tsp.) acid blend
    1 tsp. yeast nutrient
    2 Campden tablets
    ¾ tsp. grape tannin
    1 cup Madeira wine yeast starter

1. Mix all ingredients except yeast.
2. When must cools to 70°F. add yeast.
3. Ferment on pulp 7-8 days, then coarse strain, and press pulp as dry as possible. Put under fermentation lock.
4. In 3 or 4 weeks, rack and read S.G.
5. Proceed with syrup feeding. Every time S.G. falls to 1.000 add syrup to raise it to 1.010.
6. When fermentation ceases, cook in *estufa* for 3 months.
7. Fine, fortify and sweeten to taste.
8. Age 1 to 2 years in bottle.

Note: Instead of baking, this wine could be flavoured with Sherry flavour concentrate to make a "quick Sherry."

SPARKLING WINES

We describe a wine as sparkling when it contains carbon dioxide gas. The gas stays dissolved in the wine so long as it is under pressure in the bottle, but when the pressure is released it bubbles off, causing the characteristic effervescence.

Commercial sparkling wines go under such names as Crackling, Pétillant, Espumante and Champagne. The last name is rightly applied only to wine made in the Champagne district of north-eastern France.

Different sparkling wines contain different amounts of gas; pressures range from 10 lbs. per sq. in. to 90 lbs. per sq. in. The higher the pressure, the more vigorous the effervescence.

Many American sparkling wines are carbonated artificially, like soft drinks. That is, the gas is pumped in under pressure at the time of bottling. But this method requires apparatus far beyond our reach. We must make sparkling wines by bottle fermentation.

The authentic Champagne method is too difficult, but there are simpler techniques, within the scope of any experienced winemaker, that will let you make perfectly acceptable sparkling wines. I stress the word "experienced": I'm always dismayed when a man who has never made a drop of wine in his life comes along the first week in December and asks how he can make Champagne for Christmas. Wait until you have successfully made several still wines, and perhaps some sparkling cider, before you start on sparkling wines.

Method 1

This method will make any wine sparkle, whether red, rosé, or white.

1. Make a top-quality dry table wine, 10% to 11.5% alcohol by volume. This alcohol limit is important. Careful use of the hydrometer will ensure that you don't exceed it.

2. When the wine is stable and very clear, probably six months old, rack it and add 1½ ounces—no more—of sugar per gallon.

3. Immediately bottle *in Champagne bottles* (this is essential as ordinary wine bottles won't stand the pressure) with plastic stoppers properly wired down. You can buy these plastic stoppers at a winemakers' supply store.

4. Stand the bottles *upright* for 12 to 18 months.

This gives you a dry, sparkling wine with about 28 lbs. per sq. in. pressure. Each bottle will have a slight sediment. Chill the wine before serving, handle the bottles gently, and the sediment will give no trouble.

This is by far the simplest method. If you measure carefully, you should have no explosions and no flat bottles.

Method 2

Method 1 makes a dry wine. Some people will want a sweet wine, and you can make this by adding one saccharin

157

tablet to each bottle before stoppering it. Unfortunately, with some wines, saccharin gives a bitter or metallic taste.

Method 3

This is more troublesome, but yields a sweet, sparkling wine without sediment.

1. Make the basic dry table wine, 10% to 11.5% alcohol, finished, clear and stable.

2. Take 2 ounces dextrose for each gallon of wine and make it into a syrup with a little water. Thoroughly mix the wine and syrup. (*Don't* try adding more sugar to get more sparkle!)

3. To be sure of a good second fermentation, add one packet of Andovin or other good all-purpose wine yeast to the mixture and 1/4 tsp. per gallon (no more!) of yeast energizer.

4. Siphon the sweetened wine into 30-ounce soft-drink bottles and cap with crown caps. These bottles are built to stand moderate pressure.

5. Store at 65° to 70°F. Once a month, pick up each bottle, turn it upside down and then put it back upright. After 3 months all the sugar should be converted to CO_2 and alcohol. Yeast deposited on the bottom will show you that the sparkle is there. When you think the wine is ready, test one bottle. Cool it in the refrigerator, open it and see if the wine really sparkles. If so, proceed as follows. (This test, by the way, is a delightful excuse for sampling your wine early.)

6. Put the bottles in a food freezer and chill the wine to about 26°F. This usually takes 2 or 3 hours. You may see a little ice in the bottles when they are ready.

7. Get an equal number of Champagne bottles. Put into each bottle 1 ounce standard sugar syrup and 1 tablet of wine stabilizer (crushed and dissolved potassium sorbate), and put these bottles into the freezer along with the wine. (The stabilizer is essential to inhibit the yeast and prevent a third fermentation and possible explosions.)

8. When the wine is cold enough, bring out one bottle of wine and one Champagne bottle. Uncap the wine and siphon

it gently into the cold Champagne bottle, taking care to leave the sediment behind. Since the wine is so cold, it will lose very little of its gas.

9. Insert plastic stopper and wire it down.

10. Invert the bottle several times to mix the syrup and wine.

This wine will be very palatable almost immediately after bottling. Note that one ounce of syrup gives a brut (slightly sweet) wine. If you want a demi-sec (sweet) wine, use two ounces of syrup per bottle, plus the wine stabilizer tablet.

Additional Notes

These techniques will add sparkle to any sound, dry wine, but for the best possible results, make a batch of wine specially for this purpose from fruit concentrates—apricot or peach concentrate for white, cherry for rosé, or blackberry for red sparkling Burgundy.

Use Andovin or a similar high-quality all-purpose yeast that will make a firm deposit, stuck tightly to the bottom of the bottle. This obviously makes it easier to finish with a clear wine.

Fig. 31. Wine glasses. Left to right: Burgundy or all-purpose, Claret, Sherry, Rhine, Champagne.

CONCLUSION

Don't let your winemaking slip into a routine. Try these unusual wines. To be sure, they take more work and require more skill than ordinary table wines; but any winemaker who has tried them and succeeded will agree that the results are amply rewarding. The beauty of winemaking as a hobby is that it offers a never-ending challenge to your ingenuity and perseverance.

Acid Blend—a mixture of organic acids (citric, tartaric and malic in equal parts) for correcting acid deficiency of musts.

Acids—see "Total acids."

Aerobic ferment—see "Primary fermentation."

After-dinner wines—sweet, fortified wines consumed after a meal, such as Port, Muscatel, Malaga.

Aging—changes occurring in wine, after fermentation is finished, which make it a more pleasing beverage.

Alcohol—ethyl alcohol, C_2H_5OH, the preservative and intoxicating constituent of wine. Roughly half the weight of sugar in the must is converted to alcohol.

Anaerobic ferment—see "Secondary fermentation."

Antioxidant—ascorbic acid, in tablets or crystals, added to wine at time of bottling to prevent excess oxidation.

Aperitif—sweet, fortified wine drunk as an appetizer, such as Sherry, Dubonnet.

Atmosphere—14 lbs. per sq. in., sometimes used as a unit in measuring CO_2 pressure in sparkling wines. Champagne may have as much as 6 atmospheres.

Autolysis—consumption of yeast sediment by live yeast; often gives wine a bad flavour.

Balling scale—hydrometer scale indicating sugar content of must in percentage by weight.

Baster—small glass or plastic syringe, useful for taking samples of wine or must to test specific gravity, clarity or flavour.

Body—fullness of a wine, probably resulting from alcohol and glycerine content. Not related to sugar content; dry wines can be full-bodied, sweet wines can be thin.

Brix scale—same as Balling scale.

Campden tablets—7-grain tablets of potassium metabisulphite. Dissolved in must or wine, they release sulphur dioxide which acts as a sterilant and antioxidant.

Cap—floating layer of fruit pulp formed during primary fermentation.

Capping machine—hand-operated device for putting crown caps on soft-drink and beer bottles.

Capsules—plastic, lead or aluminum covers placed over corks of wine bottles to give more secure closure and to improve the appearance of the bottle.

Carbon dioxide—CO_2, the gas given off by fermenting yeast. Roughly half the weight of sugar is given off as CO_2.

Carbonation—pressure injection of carbon dioxide into beverages.

Carboy—narrow-necked glass or plastic vessel, 4 to 15 imperial gallons capacity, used with fermentation lock as secondary fermentor.

Chlorine detergent—a powerful sterilant for cleaning bottles and equipment. It kills wine yeast, so it must be rinsed off after use.

Cider—fermented apple juice, usually containing not more than 8% alcohol. May be still or sparkling, sweet or dry.

Concentrate—strained, dehydrated fruit extract, much used instead of fresh fruit for winemaking.

Cooperage—barrels, usually of white oak, for fermenting and aging wine.

Crusher—a mechanical device for breaking the skins and releasing the juice of fruit before fermentation.

Dessert wine—sweet wine, such as Sauterne or Moselle, consumed with the last course of a meal.

Dry wine—wine containing less than 1% residual (unfermented) sugar.

Energizer—nutrient added to must to increase efficiency of the yeast. Usually contains phosphates plus vitamin B.

False wine—made by adding sugar and water to the marc of first-run wine.

Fermentation lock—low-pressure valve of glass or plastic; permits escape of CO_2 from secondary fermentor, but excludes air and bacteria.

Finings—substances, such as gelatin or isinglass, which precipitate suspended matter from cloudy wine.

First-run wine—made from pure, undiluted juice of grape or other fruit.

Fixed acids—non-volatile constituents of grape and other fruit juices: malic, tartaric, citric, tannic, and phosphoric acid.

Floculation—coalescence and settling of yeast cells to a firm deposit.

Fortification—addition of distilled spirit to increase alcoholic content of wine.

Free-run wine—wine drawn from a primary fermentor without pressing the pulp.

Gallon—imperial gallon = 160 imp. fluid ounces. U.S. or reputed gallon = 128 U.S. fluid ounces, or 133 imp. fluid ounces. Check recipes and container sizes to avoid errors.

Higher alcohols—methyl alcohol, amyl alcohol, fusel oil, and other poisonous substances present in harmless amounts, if at all, in wines. May be dangerously concentrated by home distilling.

Hybrid grapes—crosses between *vinifera* and *labrusca* (European and North American) grapes.

Hydrometer—instrument for measuring density of a liquid. Essential for sugar control and many other purposes in winemaking.

Hydrometer testing jar—glass or plastic cylinder in which to float the hydrometer.

Labrusca grapes—native North American grapes with "foxy" flavour, such as Concord. Not recommended for dry or table wines.

Lees—yeast sediment in bottom of fermentation vessel.

Malo-lactic ferment—a third ferment sometimes occurring in spring when the malic acid of a grape wine is converted to lactic acid; an improvement for a high-acid wine.

Marc—pulp and juice remaining in primary fermentor when the free-run wine has been withdrawn.

Metabisulphite—sodium or potassium metabisulphite, used in winemaking to produce sulphur dioxide as a sterilant or antioxidant.

Must—crushed fruit, juice and other ingredients prior to fermentation.

Mycoderma—spoilage organism that consumes alcohol and impairs flavour of wine.

Nutrient—nitrogen-producing salts added to must to invigorate the yeast and produce more alcohol and clearer wine. Recommended for all wines except those made of pure, fresh grape juice.

Pectic enzyme—enzyme that breaks down pectin in fruit, releasing more juice, colour and flavour. Occurs naturally in overripe fruit. Should be added to all fruit musts except *vinifera* grape.

Pectin—a constituent of some fruits which tends to cause cloudiness in wine. It can be eliminated by use of pectic enzyme.

pH—a measure of acidity and alkalinity; not recommended for winemaking.

Potential alcohol—an estimate, based on sugar content of the must, of the percentage of alcohol that will be achieved in the finished wine.

Press—machine for forcing juice out of fruit pulp.

Primary fermentation—first stage of fermentation in which most yeast growth takes place, and in which air is allowed to reach the must.

Primary fermentor—open-topped vessel in which primary fermentation takes place.

Proof—a 100-degree scale for measurement of alcoholic strength of beverages, with different meanings in different countries. In Canada and Britain, 100 proof = 57.1% alcohol by volume, so 70 proof is about 40% alcohol by volume. In the U.S.A., 100 proof = 50% alcohol by volume. To avoid misunderstandings, this book describes alcoholic strength only in percentage by volume.

Racking—siphoning wine from one vessel to another, so as to leave behind the lees or sediment.

Rosé—a pink wine, neither white nor red.

Rotundifolia—a species of native American grape.

Secondary fermentation—a fermentation from which air is excluded, sometimes called anaerobic fermentation. It may continue from 2 to 6 months.

Secondary fermentor—barrel or narrow-necked vessel, fitted with a fermentation lock, in which the secondary fermentation takes place.

Second wine—see "False wine."

Shrinkage—loss of wine by evaporation from a barrel.

Sparkling wine—wine containing CO_2; effervesces when bottle is opened. May be white, red or rosé.

Specific gravity—S.G., the ratio between the density of a substance and the density of water. Unfermented musts have specific gravity higher than 1.000. Dry wines have S.G. below 1.000.

Spigot—wooden tap for drawing liquids from a barrel.

Spirits—beverages of high alcoholic content produced by distillation, such as brandy, rum, gin, whisky, vodka.

Stabilizer—sorbic acid, a non-toxic, tasteless chemical to be added when sweetening or blending the wine. Prevents renewed fermentation but will not stop active fermentation. So when most of the viable yeast has settled out or been fined out, no further fermentation will occur if sugar and sorbate are added together. It is not needed for table wines but is used for sweet and sparkling wines.

Starter—a strongly fermenting yeast culture used to start fermentation in a larger volume of must.

Sterilants—chemicals used to inhibit wild yeasts and spoilage bacteria in musts or on bottles and equipment.

Sulphiting—the use of sulphur dioxide in musts and wines, as a sterilant or anti-oxidant.

Sulphur dioxide—the gas released by Campden tablets and metabisulphites; a useful sterilant and antioxidant, tasteless and non-toxic in the recommended quantities.

Sweet wine—wine with a sweet flavour, containing 1% or more residual (unfermented) sugar.

Table wine—dry wine consumed with the main course of a meal. May be red or white.

Tannin—astringent substance found in grape pips and stems, and in oak barrels. Small quantities improve flavour and keeping qualities of wine. Essential for clearing of wine, since organic findings will not work without tannin. Must be added if deficient in wine ingredients.

Thief—the wine thief is a glass tube used to withdraw samples of wine from barrels or carboys for checking clarity and flavour.

Total acids—the amount of fixed and volatile acids in a must or wine, usually expressed in terms of citric or tartaric acid.

Topping up—the addition of wine, from a reserve supply, to keep secondary fermentors full; this minimizes oxidation of the wine.

Vinifera—the European wine grape. Grown in California, but not elsewhere in North America.

Vinous flavour—a flavour developed in mature wines made with wine yeast and grapes; it can develop in fruit wines, if good wine yeast is used.

Vinometer—instrument to measure alcoholic content of wines. Not accurate with sweet wines.

Volatile acids—acids formed in wine during fermentation, such as proprionic, acetic.

White wine—wine that is not red or rosé; may be yellow or brown.

Yeast—microscopic fungus which consumes sugar, producing alcohol and carbon dioxide. Many yeasts produce alcohol, but cultured wine yeasts make the best wine.

Yeast inhibitor—see "Stabilizer."

TABLES AND CONVERSION FORMULAS

Fluid-measure Equivalents

Note that although the U.S. and imperial fluid measures have the same names—fluid ounce, pint, quart and gallon—they differ considerably in capacity. When using recipes from other books and magazines, be sure you know which system of units the author is using.

1 imp. gallon = 160 imp. fl. ozs. = 4.5459 liters = 1.2 U.S. gallons.

1 U.S. gallon = 128 U.S. fl. ozs. = 3.7853 liters = 0.833 imp. gallon.

5 imp. gallons = 6 U.S. gallons.

1 imp. gallon of pure water weighs 10 lbs.

1 U.S. gallon of pure water weighs 8 lbs. 5.3 oz.

1 U.S. pint = 16 U.S. fluid ounces.

1 imp. pint = 20 imp. fluid ounces.

1 U.S. fl. oz. = 1.805 cubic inches = 1.041 imp. fl. oz.

1 imp. fl. oz. = 1.734 cubic inches = 0.961 U.S. fl. oz.

1 cup = 8 U.S. fl. oz. = 0.5 U.S. pint = .417 imp. pint.

Weight-measure Equivalents

U.S. and imperial weight measures are identical.

1 pound = 16 ounces = 453.592 grams = 0.45359 kilograms.

1 kilogram = 1,000 grams = 35.274 ounces = 2.2046 pounds.

1 ounce = 28.35 grams.

Temperature Equivalents

a) To convert Fahrenheit to Centigrade
   F.° −32 ÷ 1.8 = C.°

Example: To convert 68°F. to Centigrade
   68 −32 = 36
   36 ÷ 1.8 = 20
   68°F. = 20°C.

b) To convert Centigrade to Fahrenheit
   C.° × 1.8 + 32 = F.°

Example: To convert 15°C. to Fahrenheit
   15 × 1.8 = 27
   27 + 32 = 59
   15°C. = 59 °F.

Hydrometer Correction Table

A hydrometer is designed to be read at one temperature. If the must is above or below that temperature the reading will be inaccurate. The following table is for a hydrometer whose standard temperature is 59°F.

Temperature of liquid	Correction
50°F.	Subtract 0.6
59°F.	None
68°F.	Add 0.9
77°F.	Add 2
86°F.	Add 3.4
95°F.	Add 5
104°F.	Add 6.8

Example

If the temperature of the must is 95°F. and the S.G. reads 1.105, add 5 to the final figure. The correct S.G. will then be 1.110.

Proof Conversion Table

Note that "proof" is an arbitrary level of alcoholic strength, differing from one country to another. This table shows the percentage equivalents of three commonly-used proof scales.

% Absolute Alcohol by volume	Canadian Proof rating	Degrees of Proof, Sykes Scale	Equivalent U.S. Proof rating
100	75 Over Proof	175	200
97	70 O.P.	170	194
94	65 O.P.	165	188
91	60 O.P.	160	182
86	50 O.P.	150	172
80	40 O.P.	140	160
74	30 O.P.	130	148
69	20 O.P.	120	138
63	10 O.P.	110	126
57.1	PROOF	100	114.2
51	10 Under Proof	90	102
46	20 U.P.	80	92
42.5	25 U.P.	75	85
40	30 U.P.	70	80
34	40 U.P.	60	68
29	50 U.P.	50	58
23	60 U.P.	40	46
17	70 U.P.	30	34
11	80 U.P.	20	22
6	90 U.P.	10	12
0	100 U.P.	0	0

Conversion Table: *Specific Gravity at* 60°*F. to Balling*

Assuming S.G. of water at 60°F. is unity

Degrees Balling	Specific Gravity	Degrees Balling	Specific Gravity	Degrees Balling	Specific Gravity
0.00	1.000	10.0	1.039	20.0	1.081
0.50	1.002	10.5	1.041	20.5	1.084
1.00	1.004	11.0	1.043	21.0	1.086
1.50	1.006	11.5	1.045	21.5	1.088
2.00	1.008	12.0	1.048	22.0	1.090
2.50	1.010	12.5	1.050	22.5	1.093
3.00	1.012	13.0	1.052	23.0	1.095
3.50	1.014	13.5	1.054	23.5	1.097
4.00	1.016	14.0	1.056	24.0	1.099
4.50	1.017	14.5	1.058	24.5	1.102
5.00	1.019	15.0	1.059	25.0	1.104
5.50	1.021	15.5	1.062	25.5	1.106
6.00	1.023	16.0	1.064	26.0	1.109
6.50	1.025	16.5	1.066	26.5	1.111
7.00	1.027	17.0	1.068	27.0	1.113
7.50	1.029	17.5	1.070	27.5	1.116
8.00	1.031	18.0	1.072	28.0	1.118
8.50	1.033	18.5	1.075	28.5	1.120
9.00	1.035	19.0	1.077	29.0	1.123
9.50	1.037	19.5	1.079	29.5	1.125
				30.0	1.127

Specific Gravity-Potential Alcohol Table

This table shows the alcohol yield you may expect in relation to the specific gravity and sugar content of the must.

Specific Gravity	Potential alcohol by volume
1.000	0
1.005	
1.010	0.9
1.015	1.6
1.020	2.3
1.025	3.0
1.030	3.7
1.035	4.4
1.040	5.1
1.045	5.8
1.050	6.5
1.055	7.2
1.060	7.8
1.065	8.6
1.070	9.2
1.075	9.9
1.080	10.6
1.085	11.3
1.090	12.0
1.095	12.7
1.100	13.4
1.105	14.1
1.110	14.9
1.115	15.6
1.120	16.3
1.125	17.0
1.130	17.7
1.135	18.4

Note: Some published conversion tables show higher yields of alcohol than does this. But most home-made wines do not contain as much alcohol as some tables suggest, and as some winemakers seem to expect.

There is a serious disadvantage in overestimating the strength of your wine. The wine is less stable and more subject to contamination than you think it is. You are far better off to have .5% more alcohol than you had expected.

This section is for you if you have to begin winemaking in a hurry, with no time to read through the book. Someone has given you a few boxes of grapes; your plum tree has yielded a bumper crop; your children have brought home fifty pounds of blackberries. You want to get started fast, before the fruit begins to spoil.

Here's exactly what to do:

1. Get a vessel (the primary fermentor) to hold the ingredients and contain the first stage of the fermentation.

For 2-5 lbs. fruit, use a 2-gallon plastic pail.

For 15-25 lbs. fruit, use a 7-gallon plastic tub.

For 40-50 lbs. fruit, use a 12-gallon plastic tub.

For 350 lbs. grapes, use a 45-gallon oak or waxed fir barrel, or a rigid plastic drum-liner.

2. Get a square yard of sheet plastic to cover the fermentor.

3. Get the ingredients shown on the Wine Ingredients Chart which follows. Multiply or divide the quantities shown, according to the weight of fruit you have. Wine yeast, Campden tablets, yeast nutrient or energizer, pectic enzyme powder, grape tannin and acid blend may all be purchased at any winemakers' supply store. If you cannot get Andovin wine yeast, substitute a 5-gram packet of some other high-quality, ready-prepared all-purpose wine yeast.

4. Prepare the fruit as indicated on the chart.

5. Mix the ingredients, crushing the Campden tablets and stirring thoroughly to dissolve the sugar. Bring the mixture to a temperature of about 70°F. and then add the wine yeast.

6. Cover the fermentor with the plastic sheet, firmly tied down, to exclude dust and flies.

7. Now, apart from stirring the ingredients once a day, you can leave the wine alone for several days while you read through the book and find what to do next.

WINE INGREDIENTS CHART

Fruit	Weight of fruit to yield 1 gal.	Preparation of fruit	Water	Acid blend	Campden tablets
Apples	6 lbs.	Chop	1 gal.	½ oz.	1
Apricots	2½ lbs.	Destone	1 gal.	1½ tsp.	1
Blackberries	4 lbs.	Crush	1 gal.	1 tsp.	1
Blueberries	2 lbs.	Crush	1 gal.	1½ tsp.	1
Sweet cherries	3 lbs.	Crush	1 gal.	2 tsp.	1
Sour cherries	2 lbs.	Crush	1 gal.	2 tsp.	1
Cranberries	3 lbs.	Crush	1 gal.	None	1
Concord grapes	5 lbs.	Crush	1 gal.	None	1
California grapes	16 lbs.	Crush	None	1 tsp.	1
Loganberries	2 lbs.	Crush	1 gal.	1 tsp.	1
Peaches	2½ lbs.	Destone	1 gal.	1½ tsp.	1
Plums	2½ lbs.	Destone	1 gal.	1½ tsp.	1
Raspberries	2½ lbs.	Crush	1 gal.	½ tsp.	1
Strawberries	3½ lbs.	Crush	1 gal.	½ tsp.	1

Note: all teaspoon measures in this table are *level* teaspoons.

Yeast nutrient	Sugar	Raisins	Pectic enzyme	Grape tannin		Wine yeast
1 tsp.	2 lbs.	None	½ tsp.	¼ tsp.	1 pkt.	Andovin
1 tsp.	2 lbs.	None	½ tsp.	¼ tsp.	1 pkt.	Andovin
1 tsp.	2½ lbs.	None	½ tsp.	None	1 pkt.	Andovin
½ tsp. energizer	2 lbs.	1 lb.	½ tsp.	None	1 pkt.	Andovin
1 tsp.	2½ lbs.	None	½ tsp.	None	1 pkt.	Andovin
1 tsp.	2½ lbs.	None	None	None	1 pkt.	Andovin
1 tsp.	3 lbs.	1 lb.	½ tsp.	None	1 pkt.	Andovin
½ tsp.	2½ lbs.	None	½ tsp.	None	1 pkt.	Andovin
None	None	None	None	None	1 pkt.	Andovin
1 tsp.	2½ lbs.	None	½ tsp.	None	1 pkt.	Andovin
1 tsp. energizer	2 lbs.	None	½ tsp.	¼ tsp.	1 pkt.	Andovin
½ tsp.	2½ lbs.	None	½ tsp.	None	1 pkt.	Andovin
1 tsp.	2 lbs.	None	½ tsp.	None	1 pkt.	Andovin
1 tsp.	2 lbs.	None	½ tsp.	None	1 pkt.	Andovin

INDEX